The
Discovery
of
Genesis

The
Discovery
of
Genesis

How the Truths of Genesis
Were Found Hidden
in the Chinese Language

C.H. Kang and Ethel R. Nelson

Publishing House
St. Louis

Kang, C H 1895-
     The discovery of Genesis.

          Bibliography: p.
          1. Creation. 2. Bible. O.T. Genesis—Miscellanea.
3. Chinese characters—Miscellanea. I. Nelson,
Ethel R., 1923-   joint author.   II. Title.
BS650.K36   213   79-12182
ISBN 0-570-03792-1

3 4 5 6 7 8 9 10 11 12   MAL   90 89 88 87 86 85 84

TO

the memory of Liao Teck Sing, my beloved wife and companion of more than 50 years.

C. H. KANG

my daughter Laurel, sons Orlyn and Ted, and husband Roger, all of whom have encouraged me in the pursuit of this fascinating story.

ETHEL R. NELSON

CONTENTS

Foreword

There is a genuine kinship between a good detective story and this volume by The Reverend C.H. Kang and Dr. Ethel R. Nelson. The authors start with the observance of some astonishing points of correspondence between certain characters in the Chinese language and elements of the Genesis account of man's early beginnings. They go on to analyze dozens of the ideographic pictures that make up words in the Chinese language. The evidence they compile is marshaled to support the thesis that the ancient picture writing of the Chinese language embodies memories of man's earliest days. The characters when broken down into component parts time and again reflect elements of the story of God and man recorded in the early chapters of Genesis. Man and Woman, the garden, the institution of marriage, the temptation and fall, death, Noah's flood, the tower of Babel — they are all there in the tiny drawings and strokes that make up the Chinese characters.

The authors remind us that China boasts of 4,500 years of unbroken civilization. The ancient Chinese were monotheists, serving a Supreme Heavenly Ruler.

It is not out of the question that their ancient beliefs reach back to the worship of the one true God, the Creator of Genesis chapters one and two. If indeed such is the case, this book represents one of the most startling theological discoveries of the ages.

Like patient and painstaking archaeologists the authors have pieced together the evidence. Many will agree. Doubtless some will challenge their work. But there is evidence here that demands further study — that evidence cannot be ignored. That evidence cannot be brushed aside by claiming that the corresponding points between the Chinese characters and Genesis are merely the product of chance. No, this book calls for far more serious consideration.

Among the book's virtues is the fact that it can be read with appreciation and understanding by those who are neither students of language nor conversant with Chinese.

It is indeed interesting in a day when China and the United States are resuming normal relations that the language of this ancient people speaks to us in characters that are hauntingly reminiscent of the early chapters of Genesis. Perhaps God has given us a point of reference to use today in proclaiming to the Chinese themselves the full story of the entire Bible with all the richness of the Gospel of Jesus Christ.

PAUL A. ZIMMERMAN
President
Concordia Teachers College
River Forest, Illinois

Prolog ... Genesis

More than 20 years ago a small book printed in Hong Kong entitled *Genesis and the Chinese*[1] came into my possession. I found its contents more than stimulating : Chinese characters were dissected and amazingly shown to tell the stories found in the early chapters of Genesis. I reorganized the material to follow the same chronological order as the Genesis history and repeatedly used it while studying the Bible with both Thai and Chinese students during my years as a medical missionary in Bangkok, Thailand. These presentations were always accepted with considerable interest and wonder.

Later, after we again took up residence in the United States, for the purpose of the continuing education of our children, my son informed me that a friend of his at college was the grandson of the author of *Genesis and the Chinese*. It was thus that the address of this elderly Chinese minister, C. H. Kang, was obtained. He presently resides in Singapore.

Assuring Pastor Kang of the enthusiasm I had found for his project among not only Orientals but also many Occidentals, I offered to prepare his material in a new form for presentation to a wider audience. My fascination with the subject mounted as he sent a great volume of additional new characters to integrate into the manuscript.

boat

vessel

八

eight

口

mouth

I was curious to know how he happened to become devoted to delving into the mysteries of the Chinese characters. About 40 years ago in China, he explained in a letter, he had been distributing Bible portions of the Book of Genesis as a chaplain in a mission hospital. A return visit to one patient's room resulted in a confrontation with a very intelligent but puzzled Chinese lady who told him what she thought of the tract: "It is a very fine fairy tale for children but hardly worth an adult's time!" She proceeded to let him know that in her opinion educated people believe in the evolutionary theory of origins.

Our Chinese friend was embarrassed that he had, at that time, too little scientific persuasive evidence to substantiate the Genesis narrative of beginnings. He himself had always accepted it by faith — simply as the Word of God. He wrestled with the problem for days until something that he had observed in a footnote of a Mandarin textbook used by a missionary came to mind. The character 船,[2] meaning *boat*, had been analyzed as follows: 舟 a *vessel;* 八 *eight;* and 口 *mouth or person.* A comment followed that, interestingly, Noah's ark, the first great boat, had just eight passengers: Noah and his wife, with his three sons and their wives.

"If this is not a mere happenstance, there should be other Biblically relevant characters," reasoned Kang. Quickly he wrote down the character for *to create* 造, and was astonished as he analyzed the components in this figure for the first time: 土 is *dust or mud;* 口 a *mouth;* ノ the small downward stroke to the left of 土 indicates *movement or life;* and ⻌ means *able to walk.* The text in Genesis 2:7 came to his mind. "Then the Lord God formed man of *dust from the ground,* and breathed [with his *mouth*] into his nostrils the *breath of life;* and man became a living being" (not a baby but an adult, *able to walk*). Dissection of this character stimulated Pastor Kang's interest and resulted in a search which has lasted four decades.

My personal study into the history of the written Chinese language through various treatises in English found in Harvard's Chinese-Japanese Yenching Library gave its approximate time of origin as 2500 B.C. This dating is provocative, for it coincides quite closely with the time (2218 B.C.) of the great dispersion of races from the tower of Babel, as calculated from the Biblical genealogies in a recent chronological study.[3]

Discussion of this project with other missionaries from the Orient and friends precipitated some questions. How does one know that these characters are actually very ancient and not more recently contrived through the influence of Christian missionaries during the past two or three centuries, for the purpose of promoting their religious concepts? The answer to this is that very basic, fundamental, primitive, and nonreligious kinds of words are involved, including, for example: *come, go, desire, beginning, complete, first, forbidden, garden, drown, cruel, rebellion,* and scores more.

A few friends versed in the Chinese language brought up the possibility that these might be "phonetic" rather than "ideographic" characters. This point will

造
create

土
dust, mud

ノ
"p'ieh," showing life, motion

⻌
walking

be later discussed. The more ancient forms of all the characters presented have also been researched and bear out the interpretations given, oftentimes being even more explicit.

A third query has been: How does one know that the point of reference for the characters is not a pagan concept rather than a source parallel with our Scriptures? My reply to this points out that the original religion of the ancient Chinese at the time when the written language was being formulated was monotheistic in nature. They had no idols, no mythology, but worshiped a single Supreme Ruler of Heaven. The polytheistic cults of Taoism and Buddhism came about 2,000 years later. As one becomes acquainted with the study and the multiplicity of key words such as *flesh, a lord, reptile, naked, clothing, to hide, sorrow,* for example, it becomes increasingly credible that the ideographic references are to the same historical events as recorded in Genesis. But one must decide for oneself the veracity of the study.

Many long letters passed between Singapore and Stoneham, Massachusetts. When I had a rough manuscript in hand, a trip to Singapore in 1975 at long last allowed me to go over the material with Pastor Kang to our mutual satisfaction. But it was soon apparent that our study was far from complete.

Only one who has attempted to collaborate on a project such as ours can appreciate the frustrations of a 13,000 mile separation and a two-week wait for a reply to a letter. I finally realized that a second visit would be necessary in order to satisfactorily complete the thesis, and this was accomplished in the fall of 1976. This surely would be the last trip! But the end was not yet in sight. Revisions and progress were slow when mixed with both professional and homemaking careers. The summer of 1978 again found me in Singapore. On this trip I was also able to confer with Dr. Andrew Chiu, president of Concordia Seminary in Hong Kong, who enthusiastically endorsed the project.

One very difficult aspect of writing this book has been particularly challenging—to make it readable for both the creationist and evolutionist. Some explanations may appear redundant to those with a good Biblical background but are quite necessary for any who are not well acquainted with the Scriptures. A missionary would be suspect as being sympathetic with creationistic thinking, but I have really tried to remember that I also was once quite ignorant of any concepts of origins other than the evolutionary processes presented during my younger years in public school. I would not want to "turn" anyone "off" by a dogmatic or prejudiced presentation; I prefer to allow room for an honest appraisal of the subject matter introduced.

Another problem involves some new and unconventional ways of interpreting certain characters. Only those knowledgeable in the Chinese language would detect these apparent innovations. For this reason, there are explanatory study notes for each chapter. They are listed with the book references in numerical order at the end of the book. It is hoped that Chinese friends will withhold judgment until all the facts are in, for admittedly we are looking at characters in a somewhat different way. But this is not new! Many books[4] have been written in an attempt to decipher ideographically the original intent of the venerable writing, so this book is not unique except in its interpretative foundation in sacred primeval history. One's natural skepticism gives way to pondering mathematical probability when viewing the great number of characters which accurately portray these ancient sagas. Could so many meaningful ideograms "just happen" — just evolve — without intelligent synthesis?

As coauthor of C. H. Kang's thought-challenging work, I make no apologies for not being a linguist. I have learned a bit about the Chinese written language during the months of ingesting the submitted characters with their analyses. Perhaps someone, such as myself not engrained in previously accumulated knowledge and biases of the language can be more objective and critical. From the viewpoint of an English-speaking readership, something not clear to me would certainly be equally puzzling and unconvincing to others.

A most annoying experience has been trying to scrutinize a tiny printed character to identify each little stroke in its composition. Therefore a standard part of my equipment has become a three-inch magnifying glass. This is quite impractical, however, for the readers of this book, so each new character under discussion, along with its unfamiliar constituent radicals, have been greatly enlarged and placed in the margins, together with the English equivalents.

All Biblical references are from the Revised Standard Version (RSV) unless otherwise specified e.g. King James Version (KJV), New English Bible (NEB) etc. The more ancient calligraphy found in the text and notes is taken from the work of Lin Tze Ching.[5]

The outline followed in this book is intended to substantiate evidence for the truthfulness of the Genesis account, climaxed with the introduction of the heretofore unrecognized twin account of Genesis found in the Chinese characters. A brief glimpse into the ancient history and religious background is necessary first to set the stage. Then, in order to understand and appreciate the structure of the Chinese characters, a brief introduction to the written language is added to stimulate interest and launch the reader into the investigation. The body of the book follows thereafter, keeping with the Genesis chronology, as specific characters are scrutinized one by one and reduced to meaningful component parts. Very quickly the reader will begin to recognize the simpler symbols and enjoy the flavor of discovery.

There are many whom we would like to thank for their ideas, counsel given, or review of the manuscript, in whole or in part. Dr. Lit-sen Chang, special lecturer in missions at Gordon-Conwell Theological Seminary, reviewed the completed manuscript and made a number of helpful suggestions.

A special thanks is extended to Dr. E. C. Zimmerman veteran missionary to China for his careful and helpful critique of the entire completed manuscript. I would also like to mention by name others who have been most helpful at some stage in the preparation of the book: Dr. Frances Read, David Doucette, J. R. Spangler, Nancy Wall, Otho Eusey, Dr. Lynn Sauls, John Wood, Dr. Cynthia Watts, Dr. Gerard Damsteegt, Ezra Longway, Lillian Lo, and D.T. Djang.

Finally, I would like to express my great appreciation for the kindness, interest and patience of the staff of Thai Watana Panich Press Co., Ltd., Bangkok, Thailand, who have pains-takingly type-set the book with the disadvantage of working in two foreign languages—English and Chinese! Little does one realize, viewing the completed book, the separate problems they incurred in acquiring Chinese type, the services of a calligrapher, and the reproductions by their press artist of the unfamiliar ancient forms. The technology they found challenging, and the whole was accomplished without complaint!

ETHEL R. NELSON, M.D.
Pathologist
New England Memorial Hospital
Stoneham, Massachusetts

Chapter 1 : Not Without Witness

Theories of man's origin have haunted scientists and theologians alike for years. They have debated the authenticity of the beginnings of life on this earth as recorded in Genesis. Interested people the world around, it seems, have either accepted these writings "by faith" or have considered them mere fables.[1]

What would be your reaction to an extra-Biblical source of the same narratives as portrayed in the first 11 chapters of Genesis—those "hard-to-believe" early writings? One or two fragmentary stories are found in many early cultures—the creation, the fall of mankind into sin, Noah's flood—but the whole picture is not there; and vivid, accurate, unmuddied details are lacking. One might think of looking into the most ancient records and artifacts of the oldest civilization in the world for confirmation. That would lead us to China, which proudly claims the distinction of 4,500 years of unbroken civilization. But China? Who would consider this country, with its religious mixtures of ancestral worship, Taoism and its myths and magic, Buddhism and its superstitions and divinations, Confucianism and its scholarly teach-

ShangTi

emperor

above
(heavenly)

ings, as the depository of anything Judeo-Christian?

Yet, if we take a journey backward in time, passing the first century B. C., when Buddhism was introduced; the fifth century B. C., when Taoism and Confucianism simultaneously blossomed; and continue back 1,500 or even 2,000 years more, we find a different religious atmosphere. There we find the little-appreciated evidence that these ancient people served only *one* God, had *no* myths or idols, and kept a strict moral code.[2] They called their God *ShangTi* 上帝 (Shang Ti, Shang-ti, Shangti), the Heavenly *(above)* 上 *Emperor* 帝 .

It is supposed that the Chinese originally migrated from a site in Mesopotamia, for they show evidences of similarity to the later Babylo-Assyrian culture in arts, sciences, and government.[3] The approximate date of their origin, 2500 B. C., is surprisingly close to the strict chronological dating of the great event at the tower of Babel which resulted in the division of all mankind into new linguistic groups and the consequent dispersion of peoples over the face of the earth. If God at that time truly confused the mother tongues of earth, these people carried with them a newly acquired spoken language. They also must have had an accurate knowledge of historical events from the beginning of time, which they communicated by word of mouth. This should have been an accurate record, since the period spanned was only three patriarchal lifetimes: Adam to Methuselah to Shem (Genesis 5:3-32; 10:25; 11:10-16).

Because of the geographical isolation of China by mountain ranges, deserts, and oceans, this race of people was sealed off to itself, free from outside influences, as

2

it developed its own characteristic culture, nor was it disturbed for over 2,000 years.

When the Chinese, very early in their history as a separate people, found a need to communicate with a written language, a system of word-pictures was invented in keeping with the characteristic calligraphy of the ancient world. True to all primitive written languages, these so-called pictographs were satisfactory for representing objects but carried limitations in expressing abstract concepts. The early graphic symbols, therefore, were combined in meaningful ways to convey ideas, called ideograms, and these "picture stories" of necessity had to contain common knowledge in order to be understood. It would have been only natural to use as a basis for some of the ideograms the history of the ancient beginnings of humanity with which all were familiar by oral tradition. Consequently, the written Chinese language is composed of characters uniquely adapted to the possibility of containing the stories of Genesis.

We might illustrate at this point just what an ideogram is and how a concept such as the word "tempter," for example, could be translated into an expressive written character by graphically depicting the story of Eve's encounter with the devil in the Garden of Eden. In this first historic moment of temptation the devil must of course be pictured. Three primitive pictographs were selected to accomplish this: *a garden, field or landed property* 田 represents the Garden of Eden; *a man, son* 儿 shows the humanoid aspect of the devil, who spoke as a man to Eve, even though through the medium of a serpent; and the word *secret, private* 厶 conveys his

devil

man, son

garden, field

secret, private

3

clandestine approach to Eve. These three symbols, together with the "p'ieh" ノ indicating "alive," are combined in *the devil* 鬼.

But to be more specific, the *devil* 鬼 radical is then placed under the *cover* 广 of protecting *trees* 林. The *devil* 鬼 waited for Eve in the forbidden tree, which was located in the middle of the garden next to the tree of life—hence the two *trees* 林. Furthermore, he was under *cover* 广, being hidden in the tree and also camouflaged as a serpent. By uniting these primitive pictographs into an ideographic character, the word *tempter* 魔 appears to have been designed. Or were these six significant constituent symbols brought together by mere chance?

广
cover

木
tree

魔
tempter

$$ ム \ + \ 儿 \ + \ 田 \ + \ ノ \ = \ 鬼 \ + \ 林 \ + \ 广 \ = \ 魔 $$

secret	man	garden	[alive]	devil	trees	cover	tempter

The preceding serves to illustrate the purpose of this book in exploring some of the pictographic and ideographic types of Chinese characters in order to unlock what we believe is a parallel account of the fascinating chronicle of beginnings. A feature which makes this hypothesis even more tenable is that the words to be discussed in this book are of themselves very relevant to the stories of Genesis. If the inventor of the written language were seeking to portray such words by pictographs or ideographs, it would be appropriate for him to find the earliest instance in oral tradition bearing an illustration. For example: the words *bring forth, complete,* or *finish* would be expected to refer to the creation week; while *first, perfect, beginning,* and *ancestor* should apply to Adam and Eve; and *warn, covet, naked, hide,*

4

thorn, and *sorrow*, are ideas first expressed in the temptation and fall of the original human pair.

There is reason to believe that the Chinese written language bears a testimony to prehistory with emerging details closely resembling the Hebrew portrayal. Some information contained by the ancient characters gives unexpected insights into the little-understood primeval world. The graphic symbols often seem to give specifications referring to the two worlds—either that of Adam and Eve in the mysterious preflood period, or to Noah and his family, the postdiluvian (postflood) common ancestors. Most remarkable of all is that the Chinese characters have survived intact through the intervening thousands of years with very little modification in the meaning of their constituent parts, although the actual written forms have undergone stylistic changes. Today this remarkable language represents the one remaining pictographic and ideographic language in current use in the modern world.

It is the purpose of this book to propose, therefore, that the ancient Chinese people were quite familiar with the same record which the Hebrew Moses is popularly given credit for writing some 700 to 1,000 years *later*. Imagine this information being stored in special characters that were in use hundreds of years before the first page of the Bible was written! Moreover we believe that the Chinese actually employed this historical knowledge as one small facet in the process of building their written language. The significance of this claim is broad. But most important, it appears to us to give support and added acceptance to the often-slandered account of the Biblical Genesis.

5

How is it that the factuality of Genesis is now universally questioned, whereas a century ago it was generally accepted in large portions of the world? Many people today are evolutionists, having been brought up from childhood accepting this idea. Early, they are taught in school and by the media to think the earth evolved through millions or billions of years. They are frequently unacquainted with the Scriptural explanation of creation except in a fanciful or ridiculing context. This educational influence has left too many closeminded on the subject of origins, accepting only the statements of the scientific world as fact.

Thanks to archaeological finds, the credibility of the Bible is increasing.[4] Gradually, archaeologists have been digging up evidence of ancient civilizations mentioned exclusively in the Bible. Inscriptions in clay and rock have been deciphered which describe with conclusive data the very peoples once considered mere Biblical hypotheses. The 1976 find of an entire library of intact clay tablets at Tell Mardikh (ancient Ebla in Syria) by Italian archaeologists is eagerly being deciphered for meaningful associations with the early chapters of Genesis.[5] Will the early Hebrew pre-recorded history be clarified by these relic writings? Will a vast Semitic culture from the centuries prior to 2000 B.C. come to light?

There is much discussion about the origin of fossils, petrified forests, and coal and oil deposits. Do these prove evolution, or were they produced by an ancient universal flood with cataclysmic unheavals? *One* observation would meet with universal agreement: these are all remnants of a lush vegetation and vast fauna distributed worldwide, from present-day deserts to icy poles. The process which instantaneously froze, thereby preserving in toto, thousands of mammoths grazing on temperate vegetation,[6] encased ripe fruit in ice, petrified giant hardwood trees before the normal course of rotting could ensue, and liquified or carbonized other organic life into fuel for future generations must have involved the whole earth in a rapidly transpiring event.

What was the world like that nurtured these mute but splendid remnants of a former age? Each step in the process of creation is described in the first pages of Genesis as meeting God's quality-controlled perfection: "And God saw everything that He had made, and behold, it was very good" (Genesis 1:31). This primeval planet was so perfect that we can scarcely imagine how different it was from the most idyllic panorama on our present earth. We are pleased today with a much inferior familiar scene—the recovered world following the devastation of a universal catastrophe.

Terrariums have become popular in the last few years, and especially those people who have a hard time remembering to water their house plants appreciate that one can neglect the glass-encased ferns, mosses, or small-leaved plants for months at a time and see them repeatedly utilize and thrive on the meager moisture contained in the system. It has been proposed that our earth was once just such a vast enclosed greenhouse, for the great size and verdure of fossil plants suggest ideal primordial climatic conditions. A very even temperature could have been made possible by a globe-encircling vapor canopy as described in Genesis 1:6-8: "And God said, 'Let there be a firmament in the midst of the waters [originally surrounding the earth], and let it separate the waters from the waters.' And God made the firmament and separated the waters which were under the firmament [seas] from the waters which were above the firmament [water canopy]. And it was so. And God called the firmament Heaven." Also in Genesis 2:6 it is stated that a "mist went up from the earth and watered the whole face of the ground."

A water canopy encircling the earth would create an even temperature everywhere, thus eliminating winds and in turn rains. This protective vaporous mantle would also screen out harmful radiation and could conceivably contribute to the early longevity of mankind, as recorded in Genesis.[7] Truly the first world was a strangely wonderful place. But again, did it abruptly end with the emptying of the water canopy upon the earth during the universal flood? This possibility is depicted in Genesis when "all the fountains of the great deep burst forth, and the *windows of the heavens* were opened. And rain fell upon the earth forty days and forty nights" (Genesis 7:11,12). According to the Biblical record, the whole earth was convulsed in a mighty upheaval as these tumultuous waters swept away the first world's inhabitants and vegetation. Only Noah and his family, together with pairs of animal species, are recorded to have been preserved in a spacious vessel of his own making.

But how can we believe such an idealistic first world ever existed? How can we scientifically accept a "myth?" Is there any real evidence outside of fossils to substantiate the Genesis story? How about Noah's ark? Would we believe the Bible if the remnants of a mighty wooden boat, equal in dimensions to those itemized in Genesis, were found on Mt. Ararat, where this ancient vessel went aground? A number of inconclusive search expeditions to this mountain range in Turkey have been conducted over the past number of years[8].

We feel confident in presenting the material in this book that there is another reliable record of earth's beginnings which agrees in close detail with the Genesis writings. The total history of the two vastly different worlds described in Genesis will also be viewed through the eyes and creative thinking of the ancient inventor of the Chinese characters. Adam and Eve were given dominion over a perfect creation of primeval beauty, while Noah's family of eight survivors struggled to reestablish the human race in a desolate, unrecognizable and devastated land.

It is hoped that as this subject is explored, you will gain a new appreciation for earth's oldest culture and an excitement in probing the picturesque, graphic Chinese language. How miraculous that it has been preserved with so little change through the intervening millennia! Today it is still used by more of this world's populace than any other single script. Could the Chinese characters even have been divinely preserved, along with fossil remains, as supporting witnesses to the Hebrew Scriptures, which answer the perplexing question of origins?

> We . . . bring you good news, that
> you should turn from these vain things to a
> living God who made the heaven and the earth

9

and the sea and all that is in them. In past generations He allowed all the nations to walk in their own way; yet *He did not leave Himself without witness* . . . (Acts 14:15-17).

Chapter 2 : Imperial Intrigue in the Chinese Dark Ages

If we are to understand and appreciate how certain primitive Chinese characters were conceived, we must first allow our imaginations to paint an ancient scene. Envision a hardy, intelligent, and industrious people newly settling into a rugged environment of lovely valleys with serene, meandering streams and surrounding lofty mountains. These were not uncivilized barbarians, but a wise people who possessed skills in the use of metals, architecture, mathematics, and various sciences. The beauty of their natural surroundings also stimulated an inborn latent artistry. Their diversified knowledge had doubtless been acquired under the influence of their former homeland in the region of ancient Babel. The seven-day week which they used[1] could well have stemmed from their acquaintance with the history of the original creation week.

From earliest times their activities were faithfully recorded. Perhaps one of the most venerated and important manuscripts of ancient China is the *Shu Ching (Shoo King)*, the *Book of History*. This was found secreted in the wall of Confucius' house when it was pulled down in 140 B.C. Its contents, amazingly, date back nearly to the time of Noah and consist of a number of records of the first three dynasties, Hsia, Shang, and Chou, and several of their predecessors, embracing the period from the middle of the 24th century B.C. to 721 B.C.

Ancient writings had attracted the attention of Confucius when he was at the court of Chou, and selecting those things he considered valuable, he compiled the *Book of History*. It contains seeds of all things that are deemed important in the estimation of the Chinese—the foundation of their political system, their history, religious rites, basis of their tactics, music and astronomy.[2] Apparently, as these manuscripts would testify, the Chinese had an early written means of logging their annals. When and how did their writing methods come into existence?

Legends differ as to who the inventor of the written language was; however, this honor is popularly credited to Ts'ang Chieh, a minister and historian for the "yellow emperor," Hwang Ti, third ruler in the so-called legendary period of China. It is generally agreed that the rudiments of the written language came very early in the history of the Chinese as a distinct people, and by tradition this first effort at devising a pictographic and ideographic system has been assigned to about 2500 B.C.[3]

The keeping of accurate annals naturally followed in the wake of being able to chronicle events in writing. An unfailing record of successive reigning emperors has been accurately kept from the beginning of the

Hsia Dynasty in 2205 B.C. Since it is the prevailing religious climate at various periods which mainly concerns us, our brief excursion into history will center on this aspect of their culture.

For more than the past 2,000 years China has nurtured three religions: Confucianism, Taoism, and Buddhism. The Chinese, with good reason, assert that these teachings, originally three, have become one. They have temples of the Three Religions in which images of Confucius and Lao-tze (founder of Taoism) stand to the right and left of Buddha, forming a triad of sages.

The brilliant Confucius, born in 551 B.C., was a contemporary of both Lao-tze (also Lao-tse, Lao-tsze, Lao-tzu) and Gautama, the latter being the unwitting founder of Buddhism in far-off India. Confucius sifted through the records of remote antiquity and drew out those principles which he felt worthy of promotion. His models of virtue were Yao and Shun, emperors of the so-called early legendary period. He was a great reformer and moralist, became a premier of his state, and demonstrated in his own life the principles he taught. He is especially known for his pithy, wise proverbs.

Taoism is also indigenous to China. Nearly all of the gods regarded by the Chinese as overseeing their material interests originated with this sect. Theirs is a system of myths, magic, and superstition. Buddhism, which entered China about 67 B.C., is a strange paradox of religious atheism. Adherents admit to no Supreme Being but believe that the human soul is subject to endless misfortune and transmigration into different animal or human forms with the only final escape being complete extinction. The mind is withdrawn from thought and feeling by ascetic exercise, with the goal of Nirvana, a negative state of exemption from pain.[4]

But what was the religious belief in ancient China before 500 B.C. — before the age of Confucius, Lao-tze and Gautama? This intriguing history is little known or appreciated by either the Chinese or the Westerner. It was during this primeval period that the Chinese culture, as well as the language, including the beautiful and unique calligraphy, developed. As noted, court historians kept careful records, preserved from one dynasty to the next. During the first three dynasties of Hsia, Shang, and Chou, from c. 2205 to 255 B.C., the Supreme Heavenly Ruler, *ShangTi*, 上帝 also designated as *T'ien* (Heaven), 天, and occasionally *Shen* (God, a spirit), 神, was venerated. In fact, the Chinese were *monotheists* in an ancient world of polytheistic worship.

The earliest account of religious worship, found in the *Shu Ching* (the *Book of History* compiled by Confucius), records of Emperor Shun in 2230 B.C., "He sacrificed to ShangTi." This ceremony had reference to what became known as the "border sacrifices" because at the summer solstice the emperor took part in ceremonies to the earth on the *northern border* of the country, while at the winter solstice he offered a sacrifice to heaven on the *southern border*. Wrote Confucius in the *Chung Yung*, "The ceremonies of the celestial and terrestrial sacrifices are those by which men serve *ShangTi*."[5]

上帝
ShangTi,
Heavenly
Ruler

天
Heaven

神
God, a
Spirit

14

But can *ShangTi* be identified as the same Supreme Being of Genesis? Let us examine portions of the recitation script from the annual border rituals in which the emperor, as high priest, alone participated in the sacrificial service:

Of old in the beginning, there was the great chaos, without form and dark. The five elements [planets] had not begun to revolve, nor the sun and the moon to shine. In the midst thereof there existed neither forms nor sound. Thou, O spiritual Sovereign [神皇], camest forth in Thy presidency, and first didst divide the grosser parts from the purer. Thou madest heaven; Thou madest earth; Thou madest man. All things with their reproducing power got their being.[6]

This recitation extolling *ShangTi* as Creator of heaven and earth sounds surprisingly like the first chapter of Genesis. "In the beginning God created the heavens and the earth. The earth was without form and void, and darkness was upon the face of the deep . . . "(Genesis 1:1, 2. Read the entire first chapter). Furthermore, the Chinese must have had a sense of love, kinship, and filial feeling for *ShangTi* as the Emperor continued:

Thou hast vouchsafed, O *Ti* [帝], to hear us, for Thou regardest us as a *Father*. I, Thy child, dull and unenlightened, am unable to show forth my dutiful feelings.[7] [Italics supplied.]

The Heavenly Ruler is praised for his loving kindness as the ceremony concludes:

. . . Thy sovereign goodness is infinite. As
a potter, Thou hast made all living things. Thy
sovereign goodness is infinite. Great and
small are sheltered [by Thy love]. As engraven
on the heart of Thy poor servant is the sense
of Thy goodness, so that my feeling cannot
be fully displayed. With great kindness Thou
dost bear with us, and not withstanding our
demerits, dost grant us life and prosperity.[8]
[Italics supplied.]

These last two recitations, taken together, bear
the same simile as found in Isaiah:

But now, O Lord, Thou art our *Father; we are
the clay, and Thou our Potter* and we all are
the work of Thy hand (Isaiah 64:8 KJV).

Veneration of the ancestors was an early innova-
tion, possibly derived from the practice of the emperor
acting as high priest in the worship of *Shang Ti.* Here
was the first intercessor between God and man in
China. With the death of the earthly royal intercessor,
his spirit was believed to continue in mediatorial
service. At first emperors, then later national heros,
and finally family patriarchs were revered—not as
deities but as spirit intercessors who could grant favors
and take an interest in the current welfare and future
benefit of the suppliant.

The concept of ancestor worship antedated Confucius and is still above all other ties for both families
and communities. At death, graves of the mighty
were filled with terracotta models of horses, carts,
houses, furniture, and slaves for the use of the deceased.
The most extravagant burial of all time was that of the

great conqueror Ch'in Shih Huang-ti, who in 209 B.C. was buried beneath a great artificial mound, 500 feet high and two miles in circumference. The complex of subterranean passages was filled with untold treasures. Ten thousand workmen employed in its construction were entombed with him.[9]

Only today is this mammoth 2,200-year-old burying ground being explored by Chinese archaeologists, who estimate its complete retinue of life-sized pottery soldiers and horses guarding the resting emperor number about 6,000. Building on this immense mausoleum began when the king ascended the throne at the age of 13 and continued for 36 years, utilizing the services of some 700,000 slave artisans. Excavations begun in 1974 have not yet reached the emperor's tomb, and already the finds are breathtaking.[10]

But why should we go into detail concerning the single emperor, Ch'in Shih Huang-ti? It is because *his reign was pivotal not only for the establishment of the Chinese empire but also from the standpoint of the religious course of the empire.* The youthful Ch'in Shih Huang-ti came to the throne of the Ch'in dynasty in 246 B. C., and within 25 years had conquered all of China's separate warring states, thus unifying the great nation. He then declared himself the "first universal emperor." The name "China" is derived from his dynastic appellation. He was noted for many accomplishments, among them the completion of the Great Wall, which extends like an endless, undulating serpent for 1,500 miles. He built roads, a vast canal system, *standardized the style of writing the Chinese characters*, as well as weights and measurements. He is especially noted for having burned the ancient classics and records, and for burying alive over 400 Confucian scholars who opposed his violent "reforms."[11]

Although a ruthless executioner of the Confucianists, he apparently fell under the influence of Taoist superstitions and allowed corruption of the ancient"border" sacrifices to *ShangTi* and the erection of an additional four altars to the white, green, yellow, and red *"Tis"* (heavenly rulers).

With the death of Ch'in Shih Huang-ti, the Ch'in dynasty, lasting only 49 years, ended and the new Han dynasty followed. A famous Taoist, Sin Hwan-p'ing, influenced a Han emperor, Wan by name, in 166 B.C., to offer the first imperial sacrifices to the additional spurious *Tis*, contrary to the teachings of antiquity. *Thus a polytheistic service supplanted the original worship of the one God, ShangTi.* Because of this meddling with the ancient rites, the chief of censors accused Sin Hwanp' ing of treason, writing in a memorial:

> I venture to say that nothing is more foolish than this new figment of the spirits *ShangTi*, of which he says that there are five. It is indeed certain, that from the most ancient times, all who have been wise, and deemed masters of the nation, on account of their reputation for distinguished wisdom, have known but one *ShangTi*, eminent over all, on whom all things depend, from whom is to be sought whatever is for the advantage of the empire, and to whom it is the duty and custom of the emperors to sacrifice.[12]

Not long after the presentation of this memorial, Sin Hwan-p'ing was put to death, but the corrupt practice continued on unchanged *for more than 12 centuries.*[13]

During the Ming dynasty an investigation was carried out regarding the imperial sacrificial system. Two committees of historians were appointed about A.D. 1369 to delve into the existing ancient records to ascertain the original rituals. By so doing, they discovered the Taoist-inspired error and deviation from the original ritual of the first three dynasties of Hsia, Shang, and Chou (2205–255 B. C.). They abolished these practices and returned once again to the ritual of Chou, by which the emperor worshiped a solitary heavenly ruler, *ShangTi.*[14]

So it appears that the primitive religion of China was monotheistic with worship of a heavenly Creator and living God whose benevolent blessing was sought by the emperor as high priest and by the mediatorial invocation of worthy deceased ancestors. However, *with the introduction of Taoist and Buddhist concepts, all original meaning of their rituals was lost and religious appellations were falsely applied to expanding mystical ideas of spirit deities.* Many ancient records had been burned, and religious worship was altered, revised, and blurred with the passage of time.

Over a hundred years ago, as the Bible was being translated into Chinese by Protestant missionaries, debate arose among them as to what Chinese term should be used for "God" *(Elohim, Jehovah, Theos).* With the research that emanated on the subject at this time, a real appreciation resulted for the original religious concepts of the Chinese. They found that, in truth, the ancient

19

Chinese worshiped a God of Heaven with attributes identical to those of the Christians' deity. Declared one distinguished translator of the Chinese classics:

> Do the Chinese know the true God? . . . The evidence supplied by Chinese literature and history appears to me so strong, that I find it difficult to conceive how anyone, who has studied it, can come to the opposite conclusion.[15]

Shen, God

This same researcher into the Chinese religion declared:

> Have ever the Chinese, during the four thousand years over which their history extends, fashioned an image of *ShangTi*? They have not. *ShangTi* is self-existent. He existed before the heaven and the earth and sun. He created them. He rules over them. His years have no end.[16]

ShangTi, God

The terms decided upon to designate "God" in the Chinese versions of the Bible are *Shen*[17] 神 and *Shang-Ti* 上帝, and for the Holy Spirit *Sheng Ling* 聖靈, this latter a Christian combination of two ancient characters: *holy* 聖 and *spirit* 靈.

Sheng Ling, Holy Spirit

In summary, we find that *the written language of China was conceived during the primeval, monotheistic period*, when the religious concepts were still pristine and the history of earlier ages unmuddied by later innovations. This ancient pictographic and ideographic language has survived unscathed, and we believe bears a witness to the original beliefs of the Chinese, handed down by oral tradition. The record contained by many specific characters carries such a close similarity to the

Hebrew Genesis that it would seem only logical to believe that both civilizations must have access to the same common historical knowledge. Acquaintance with the true early religious background of the Chinese therefore makes Genesis correlation more credible and understandable.

Chapter 3: Easy Lessons in "Character Building"

The Occidental is rightly awed when looking at the written Chinese language. Whereas the Western alphabet has a mere 26 letters from which to make thousands of combinations forming words, long and short, ordinary or exotic, colloquial or erudite, the Chinese language has a far more complex and intriguing system.

For our purpose, we will study the written language quite superficially and quickly find how it builds on itself. Be assured that the ordinary careful reader will not find this baffling or too difficult to comprehend. However, it is necessary to have a basic introduction to the Chinese characters which will be not only informative but also interesting.

All ancient script began with simple line drawings of familiar objects. Word picture systems were developed by many civilizations including the early Sumerian people in the Mesopotamian Valley, the Egyptians, and the Chinese. In the evolution of most scripts, ideograms emerged at the demand for more abstract ideas of size, movement, thought, and feeling, a feature of the Chinese language that will be demonstrated in this chapter. Since the pictographs and ideographs had corresponding sounds of the spoken language, they were also phonetic. The more cumbersome drawings of most early languages were abbreviated into shortened forms for the sake of rapid writing until letters evolved and phonetic alphabets were born. This latter simplified writing, however, never developed in the Chinese language.

Only in the past few decades have actual changes been fostered in Chinese writing in an attempt to simplify the characters and make reading and writing easier. These modifications completely destroy the pictographic aspects of the language. Therefore in the near future the classical Chinese characters may be as dead as ancient Latin or Greek. Instead of being the written language of the greatest number of people on the face of the earth today this venerable writing may fall into disuse and be known and studied only by scholars.

Whereas most written languages construct words from the letters of an alphabet, the Chinese written language uses *radicals*, also called *keys, roots* or *primitives*, as the basic units and building blocks for the word characters. Each character contains one or more *root* symbols. The *radicals*, of which there are 214, are in turn organized according to the number of strokes required in writing them, anywhere from one to 17. Numbered in definite order[1], from the simplest to the most complex, these *keys* must be memorized in proper sequence by the scholar so that they may be recited easily.

The *radicals* are the most *primitive* (hence this synonym) form of the language and many are clearly pictographs, or word pictures; for example, *a cliff of preci-*

23

厂
cliff

宀
roof, house

巛 川
*streams,
to flow*

爪
claws, to grasp

田
field, garden

木
tree

口
*mouth,
person*

罒 网
net

火 灬
fire

彡
hair

羽
wings

pice 厂 obviously is an embankment; *a roof or house* 宀 demonstrates a gable in the center with eaves at the edges; *streams, to flow* 巛 or 川 , show torrents or eddies of moving water; *claws of birds or animals, to scratch or grasp* 爪 , depicts digits spread apart in such a way that the extremity is poised for action.

As this book is read, one will become fascinated at the ingenuity demonstrated in the language. Because the objects represented are so graphic, many of the radicals are easy to remember. *Field, landed property, garden* 田 looks, like a well-marked-out and irrigated plot of land. *A tree, wood or wooden* 木, shows not only the tree (the vertical line above the horizontal line of the ground), but also branching roots. *Mouth, speech, talk* 口 is in fact a gaping orifice and can represent not only the oral cavity but also the activities of the mouth such as eating, speaking, or breathing. Just as in English one uses the expression "so many mouths to feed" in reference to the number of individuals indicated, so 口 can also represent a person.

A net, 网 or 罒 , is surely a trap through which a fish could never pass. One need hardly be told that 火 or 灬 is *fire*, for either the flames leap upward in the first symbol, or lick along the ground in the second. *Hair, feathers,* are illustrated by 彡 , which appear like long combed tresses, while 羽 , *feathers, or wings,* very similar to 彡 , show the plumage attached to a pair of wings.

There are a number of radicals used to represent *a man.* The most simple is a vertical stroke 丨 . Slightly more developed is 儿, a key which pictures a trunk with

24

the left leg slightly angulated (as viewed from behind), and the right one stretched out for walking. A third symbol for *man, person, or mankind* is 人, with both legs spread apart, This last primitive has a second form 亻, which is merely a lateral compression of 人.

man, person

A simple horizontal stroke — can mean *heaven, or earth or one*, depending upon its relative position. The numeral *one* is written in the middle of a character or radical; *earth* at the base; and *heaven* at the top. The first three numerals are readily apparent: *one* —, *two* 二, and *three* 三. *Ten* is 十. When *one* — *man* | stands on the *ground* —, his *ten* 十 toes are placed on the *earth* 土, and this symbol becomes the word *dirt, mud, dust, soil, clay*. This brief introduction serves to illustrate the truly pictorial aspect of the language as depicted by the preceding primitive radicals.

heaven,
earth, one

二
two

三
three

十
ten

The formation of more complex radicals or characters by combining radicals is next demonstrated in a simple way. By using the basic symbol 人 for *man*, many new words were developed. Add to the *man* 人 radical a horizontal stroke, *one* —, so that it looks like a man with arms outstretched, 大, and the word become an ideographic radical with the suggestion of being *great, big, tall*, or in reference to man, *noble, high in rank, or full grown*. When a man grows old, he uses a cane, as if three-legged. The character then is written 太 and carries the superlative meaning of *very, much, too, or excessive*.

dust, dirt

man

大
great, noble

When a man is grown and married, he is pictured as having a second person with him. Literally he is "*two* 二 *men* 人" and no longer single. A *husband* is

very, much

25

夫

husband,
distinguished
person

失

to lose

天

heavens

therefore depicted as 夫. In the Orient, when the husband loses his wife by death, he grows a beard or moustache for several months as a sign of mourning. The word *husband* may also show a "mourning badge" as 失 demonstrates a small stroke added to the left. This alteration forms an ideogram signifying *to lose·* Since the small stroke is attached to the upper "second" man of *husband* 失, it indicates the *loss* or cancellation of *one*.

The position of the horizontal strokes is important· *Husband* is 夫, but if the upper horizontal stroke is placed at the top of the figure, 天, this designates *heavens, firmament, or sky,* since nothing is higher than the "sky." Thus 太, 夫, 失, and 天 are all characters built upon radical 37 大, which in turn is formed from radical 9 人.[1]

At this point it should also be noted that Chinese characters are formed in such a way that they have the familiar configuration of a square. Therefore the constituent radicals may be stretched out or squeezed together in order to conform to a given space in the total figure. For artistry's sake, vertical or horizontal lines of adjacent radicals in a character are lined up as in 鬼, or merged as in 我, a combination of 手 and 戈. The base of one radical may become the top of another so there need be no repetition of lines, as in 商, where and 立, 几 and 冂 share the same horizontal stroke.

Two or more simple pictographs joined together express an entirely new idea, giving birth to an ideograph. To illustrate, here are some samples:

26

舌, *tongue*, is a protrusion from the *mouth* 口 and is composed of *thousand* 千 and *mouth* 口. Note the "p'ieh" at the top of the figure ノ to indicate the *thousand* "movements" of the tongue.

舌

tongue

千

thousand

言, *words, speech, to talk,* are formed by vapor or breath rising from the *mouth.*

言

words

侶, a *companion or mate,* uses 口 to mean a *person.* Two *persons* joined together are *mates* 呂 and when qualified with *man* 亻 indicate *human companions.*

侶

mate

旦, *dawn or morning* sees the *sun* 日 emerging above the horizon of the *earth* 一.

旦

dawn

Most of the characters selected for this book are exact and clever in their structure. They reveal the philosophy and wit of the inventors of the language and are worthy of our careful scrutiny. Time is needed to study, appreciate, and learn the Chinese characters so beautifully preserved from antiquity. They provide enough material to preach a hundred sermons to all people still occupying the earth more than 4,000 years later.

The characters with which we will be dealing in this book are very ancient, but through the past 2,000 years there has been scarcely any change in their constituent radicals, since the identical characters are also used in the other Oriental countries, such as Japan and Korea.[2]

The possibility of alterations in these Chinese words through a Christian influence is also negated since the characters were well established before Christians entered China. The earliest record of any Christian mission to China is found inscribed on the Nestorian monument in Sianfu, erected in A. D. 781. Sianfu was the capital of the T'ang empire (A. D. 618-906) and the center of the then-greatest civilization in the world. This monument recorded the visit to the T'ang court of a band of Christians led by Alopen from Ta-chin (Syria). Alopen brought with him the "true scriptures." They were given to Emperor T'ang T'ai-tsung who commanded that they be translated in the royal library. These Christians flourished under royal sponsorship until A.D. 845, when they suffered persecution, and soon afterward, neared extinction.

In 1908 other Christian documents were discovered in a rock cavern a thousand miles to the west of Sianfu in the desert. Sir Aurel Stein, a British archaeologist, purchased these ancient manuscripts, one of which was dated A.D. 641, and is thus the oldest Chinese translation of any gospel portion. It is thought that these documents were written by the same Christian group as those in Sianfu.[3]

In spite of these early visits to China by Christian missionaries, the Chinese written language containing the primitive words used in this book had already been disseminated to other Oriental countries. Thus it is not the Christian influence which brought a knowledge of the history of the Genesis account to China, but this information must have been known thousands of years earlier when the language was first invented.

A partial classification of the characters is here outlined in order to introduce the novice to the clever mechanics of the language. An acquaintance with this classification is also necessary to understand the thesis and claims of this book.

I. *Pictographs.* These are thought to be the most primitive symbols, of which there are about 600 in number. Examples are ⊙ *the sun,* later modified to 日 ; and 馬 *a horse.* The 214 radicals are largely from this pictographic group. As has been stated previously, the radicals are the building blocks; for one or more are used to compose every more complex character in the language.

日
sun

馬
horse

II. *Ideographs.* Two or more simple characters are united to give a new idea. Ideographs form a very important step in the development of the language. As one linguist said, "Of the time when these characters were invented, we know nothing; but it is plain that their introduction must have given a very extended scope to the language, and they offer an interesting study, as, *in many instances, giving us an insight into the moral and social conditions of those who framed them.* [Italics supplied.] For example, if we analyze the character 信, meaning *sincere* [*trustful*], we find that it is formed by the combination of the characters of 亻 *a man* and 言 *words,* a collocation of ideas which speaks well for the honourable truthfulness of the ancient Chinese." There are about 700 ideographs.

sincere

man

言
words

III. *Phonetic characters.* These are formed from radicals being brought together for their sound rather than meaning. There are about 20,000 of these, accounting for the greatest number of written words. When the Chinese began to apply phonetic principles, the written language expanded rapidly. Each character of this type consists of two parts, a signific radical and a phonetic portion. The former gives in a general way something of the meaning of the character, while the latter suggests its pronunciation.[4]

This is an example of how such a phonetic character is formed. The Chinese colloquial word for *mother* is "ma." In order to develop a character for this word, the coiner of the new character chose a common phonetic radical possessing the sound, "ma," 馬 *a horse*, and combined this with the radical 女 for *woman*. Thus the new character 媽 means a *mother*, but not a *horse woman*. In other words, the phonetic portion no longer has pictographic or ideographic meaning, and therefore one analyzing the character from its constituent parts would not understand it. The structure of many of these characters in use today is obscure since the phonetic aspect of Chinese has changed drastically during the intervening millennia.

mother

woman

馬

horse

There is a point of controversy among linguists as to whether some characters are ideographic and whether the constituent radicals were intended to be literally translated or phonetic, with part of the components used only for sound and not for meaning. Since with the passage of time the original sound of the phonetic has been lost through regional modifications in dialectic changes, large numbers of characters are left with neither ideographic nor phonetic meaning. Hence their composition appears haphazard and devoid of practical sense today. In other words, the majority of Chinese characters do not tell a story and if "translated" would be quite nonsensical.

It should be said at this point that the characters dis-
cussed in this book are believed to be either pictographs
(Class I) or true ideograms (Class II), since their consti-
tuent radicals appear to have been carefully selected by
the inventor to convey a specific thought. Most of these
characters are also fairly simple, which in itself suggests
a primitive origin. If it is argued that these selected
characters are mere phonetic combinations, it would seem
that the possibility of chance formation of completely
meaningful words from almost limitless happenstance
phonetic possibilities is mathematically narrowed with
each additional radical contained. The likelihood of thus
producing a random intelligent ideogram, especially
applicable to a specific Genesis story, might be compared
to the proverbial explosion in a print shop resulting in the
fortuitous compilation of English words![5]

Earliest identified inscriptions have been found on
oracle scapular bones and tortoise shells, which were
used for divination purposes during the Shan dynasty
(1766—1122 B. C.) The Supreme God was thus con-
sulted regarding every act of life from the propitious
time for planting to royal troop movements. The most
ancient forms of writing are also found on large numbers
of bronze vessels and pottery, as well as stone and jade
carvings. Even during the Shang dynasty there were
already some 5,000 different characters, both pictographs
and ideographs.[6]

The Chinese were greatly concerned with writing,
and it bore an intimate relationship to the arts and paint-
ing. The Chinese were the inventors of paper about
A. D. 100; had the first Chinese dictionary in A. D.
121, containing 9,353 characters; invented block print-

ing in the 9th century; the movable press in the 11th century; and prior to 1750 had printed more books than the rest of the world put together! It is no wonder then that their estimation of "civilization" (wen hua) is literally, "the transforming influence of writing," while the English word "civilization" refers to urbanization as a sign of being civilized.[7]

[Seal]

There are several different forms or styles of scripts in which Chinese characters may be written, and although all of these calligraphies are very old, they are still in use today for designated purposes.

[Square]

There are two types of antique seal characters: the *greater seal characters* are ascribed to a court historian, Shin Chou, about 900 B. C., and were created to take the place of the simple pictographs found on early bronzes and ancient drums. The *lesser seal characters* are said to have been used by Li Ssu, a minister of the great "First Emperor," Ch'in Shih Huang-ti, in the Ch'in dynasty, about 240 B. C., for the purpose of unifying writing.[8] These seal scripts are used today only for ornamental purposes, and upon public and private seals.

[Grass]

The *Li is a square character*, introduced about 200 B. C., now used only on scrolls, fans, and stone tablets. About A. D. 350, during the Tsin dynasty, the *Ts'ao, Grass or Rapid style* was introduced, taking its name from the straw paper that it was first used upon. Today is used only for scrolls or on paintings.

[Printers']

A form used by *printers* in books was developed during the Sung dynasty A. D. 960—1279. The *Cursive, or Running hand* was first used during the T'ang dynasty

[Cursive]

A. D. 618—906, and has been in common use for hand-writing and bookkeeping ever since.[9]

Besides unifying the written language of China through the use of the lesser seal characters, Ch'in Shih Huang-ti's prime minister, Li Ssu, was also given the task of listing the then-known characters. This original catalog, produced in 213 B. C., contained about 3,000 words, The creation of new pictographic radicals had ceased before 800 B. C., and the phonetic principle was already in use for inventing new characters by combining the radicals.

The first etymological (word origin) studies in Chinese are attributed to Hsu Shen (86 B. C.), who used Li Ssu's catalog and produced the *Shuo Wen*. Hsu Shen thus attempted to explain for the first time possible derivations of nearly 8,000 characters.[10]

By this time in the course of history, ideas of Taoism had already become firmly rooted in Chinese thinking. The original religion, known and understood 2,000 years before at the time when the writing was first invented, had become nearly extinct. Naturally Hsu Shen's interpretations of certain characters would be in the light of his own knowledge and belief. Even today the *Shuo Wen* is the basis of most modern interpretations and analyses of Chinese writing.

We would like to introduce an entirely different etymological interpretation, of applicable characters, based upon primeval history as found in Genesis, which was no doubt known to the ancient Chinese monotheists by oral tradition. This, from a historical perspective, would appear to be a more logical foundation of analysis for some of the simplest and most primitive radicals and characters. Occasionally the more ancient forms portray specific details lacking in today's "modern," 2,000-year-old traditional characters. Therefore, in order to clarify or substantiate an interpretation, a few of these unique older stylized figures will be included.

So, in summary, we find that the written Chinese language had its origin about 2500 B. C., shortly after the migration of the future Oriental people from the vicinity of ancient Babel. This point in time corresponds quite closely to the genealogical date of the dispersion of Genesis 11 (c. 2218 B.C. See p. ix). Thus *The Discovery of Genesis* has good foundation in chronological, historical, and geographical fact. The next chapter will begin a study of selected meaningful characters comparing them with the Genesis narrative.

Chapter 4 : Creation — Chinese Style

Since the advent of modern technology and the computer, it is perhaps easier for us to begin to comprehend how God's creative acts might have been instantaneously accomplished. A single spoken word by God, such as "dog," was promptly translated into an adult animal of given size, with fur, head, tail, and all anatomy complete and specific for a dog down to the last cell. Its brain was canine; its voice was characteristic of this creature, with a growling, barking, and whining "vocabulary" already built into the cerebral convolutions. We might say that God had "programed" each object of creation to the last detail, so that it took only a spark of creative energy in a word to bring it into being.

The opening words of Genesis record: "The earth was without form and void, and darkness was upon the face of the deep" (Genesis 1: 2). Out of the emptiness and darkness of this initially water-covered, terrestrial ball came perfection and beauty. On successive days light, the firmament, dry land and seas, vegetation bearing seed, the luminaries of the heavens, birds, fishes, and mammals came forth at His fiat. He thereby converted

His measureless energy, expressed as a command, into mass, or created objects, following an elementary law of nature: Mass and energy can neither be created nor destroyed, but energy can be converted into mass, or mass into energy. "For *He spoke*, and *it came to be: He commanded*, and *it stood forth*" (Psalm 33:9).

God

示
示
礻

*proclaim,
manifest,
exhibit,
reveal,
(the "God"
radicals)*

One of the words for *God*, a Spirit, is written 神 Let us look at the radical on the left 礻, for it bears on the creation story. This portion may be written in three forms: 示, 示, or 礻. The first of these, 示, may be written alone and conveys the meaning *to proclaim, to exhibit, to manifest, reveal.* Surely God did these as He performed His creative work. The Gospel of John in the New Testament comments on the Creatorship: "In the beginning was the Word, and the Word was with God, and the Word was God. ... All things were made through Him, and without Him was not anything made that was made. ... And the Word became flesh and dwelt among us" (John 1:1, 3, 14). The Creator is called the "Word," for His creative power was *manifested* by His command, which was simply, "Let there be," and it was so.

"God" in the original Hebrew of Genesis is *Elohim*, a plural term used for the multiple aspects or personalities of God. These are more clearly developed in the New Testament as the Father, the Son, and the Holy Spirit (Matthew 28:19). "The Word [that] became flesh and dwelt among us" is obviously a reference to the Son, Jesus.

Very early, in the second verse of Genesis 1, as the creative activity on our earth was begun, the agent in

36

all this tremendous work during the first momentous week is identified: "The earth was without form and void, and darkness was upon the face of the deep; and the *Spirit of God* was moving over the face of the waters" (Genesis 1:2). Let us examine closely the word for *Spirit* 靈, which has compacted into its strokes much information about the three members of the Godhead, and especially the assignment of the Holy Spirit. This character is made up of three smaller units: 乕, 口 口 口, and 巫. Each will be considered in turn with a more complete dissection.

Spirit

cover

Let us first examine 乕. The horizontal stroke at the top of the figure, because of its position, represents *heaven* and indicates where the Spirit came from. The second horizontal stroke ⌐ means *cover*. The remaining portion of the figure, as expected, is *water* 冫. (This radical is usually written as 水 or 氵, but an ancient form is 巛). 乕 is therefore an exact picture of Genesis 1:2, "the Spirit of God was moving over the face of the waters," which describes the first descent of God's Spirit to this earth. The entire radical 乕, a second form being 雨, means *rain*. This is also significant symbolism for the theologian.[1]

water

rain

The next portion of the word for *Spirit* is 口 口 口, *mouth*, three in number. These radicals imply that three persons are speaking via the Spirit. This agrees with the New Testament teaching on the Trinity. Jesus told His disciples regarding the office of the Holy Spirit, "But when the Counselor comes, *whom I shall send to you from the Father*, even the *Spirit* of truth, who proceeds from the Father, *He will bear witness to Me*"(John 15:26).

mouth

instead of,
substitute

distinguished
person, sage

to speak

conduct

靈

Spirit

工

work

man

巫

worker of
magic

The Spirit of God is an ambassador of the Father and Son, representing their mouths as well as His own, making three. This claim can be verified by a separate character meaning *instead of, or to substitute* 替. Here is seen the radical *to speak* 曰, and above it two *distinguished person(s)*夫. It is apparent that the *speaker* 曰 is a spokesman not only for himself, but for the two other *respected persons*夫夫 as well, making three, for he speaks instead of or as a substitute. This parallels the 口 口 口 *mouths*. Most importantly, the acts of creation were performed by *speaking* things into existence. "By the *word* of the Lord the heavens were made, and all their host by the *breath of His mouth*" (Psalm 33: 6).

Interestingly, the three mouths written as an independent word in a different form 品 mean *conduct or actions*. Supposedly the ancient Chinese accepted the words spoken by the three mouths with authority as their rule of conduct.

The final component of *Spirit*, written 亚, is made up of three radicals, 人工人, signifying *man, work, man*. Notice also that a third *man* 丨 is inside the word *work* 工.[2] In its original composition, the upper horizontal stroke represented *heaven*, while the one at the base indicated the *earth*. The vertical stroke joining them together depicted a person *working*. Therefore, there are really three persons working together under heaven upon the earth 人 丨 人, illustrating again the concept of three personages operating together in the creation of the earth. Three *men* 人 丨 人 have three *mouths* 口 口 口.

However the whole character 亚 means a *worker of magic*. What more descriptive title could be given to the Spirit of God in that first week of creation? "By faith we understand that the world was created by the *word* of God, so that *what is seen was made out of things which do not appear*" (Hebrews 11:3). Today the Chinese also apply this word 巫 to a *witch, wizard, or one devil-possessed.* What a pity that the spirit of the devil has replaced the Spirit of God in the interpretation of this symbol!

As one contemplates the entire character for the *Spirit* 靈,[3] one might well marvel at its composition. This word alone profoundly reveals the history of the Spirit of God: His "moving upon the face of the deep" at the time of creation, and His work through the different ages as the representative of the God-head to this earth. This would seem to indicate that the Chinese had a true concept of the Trinity.

一 + 冖 + ∷ = 零 + 口 口 口 + 巫 = 靈
heaven   cover   water   rain   three   worker   Spirit
person   of magic

Spirit

According to the Biblical record the entire creative work of bringing our earth from a chaotic state to Edenic beauty and completion took but six days. There is today considerable controversy about the length of these so-called "days." Just how long were they? The creation week had started with day one when "God said, 'Let there be light'; and there was light. And God saw that the light was good; and God *separated the light from the darkness.* God called the light *Day*, and the darkness He called *Night*. And there was *evening* and there was *morning, one day*" (Genesis 1: 3-5). The word "day" here in Hebrew is *yom*, used everywhere else in the Old Testament for an ordinary day.

During the second day the water encircling the earth was divided so that the atmosphere with life-supporting gases was formed. "God said, 'Let there be a vault between the waters, to separate water from water.' So God made the vault, and separated the water under the vault from the water above it, and so it was; and God called the vault heaven" (Genesis 1:6-8, NEB).

生

to bring forth

On the third day, "God said, 'Let the waters under the heavens be gathered together into one place, and let the dry land appear" (Genesis 1:9). After God restrained the seas into "one place" so that the earth's soil was exposed, vegetation was *brought forth* 生.[4] Note the three positions of the horizontal strokes of 生, indicating that not only plants and animals were *brought forth* from the *earth*, but also marine life and vegetation in the *sea*, and birds and created objects in the *heavens*. The "p'ieh" ノ on the left of the figure indicates activity or life. These remaining works of creation God accomplished on the fourth, fifth, and sixth days of this first week, by speaking them into being.

By the sixth day the earth was ready for the most important miracle of all—the creation of man. God had spoken into existence the beautiful earth and its animal inhabitants. The creation of man was to be different. Let us see if the Chinese linguistic record bears out the Biblical story relating that it was with special loving care that "the Lord God *formed man* of *dust from the ground* and *breathed* into his nostrils the *breath of life*; and man became a *living being*" (Genesis 2:7).

The word *to create, to begin, from* 造, has forever memorialized that crowning work of shaping the first man. Adam from the dust of the earth. That this word 造 refers exclusively to the creation of Adam and not to the other plant and animal life will become apparent. One can see the very activity of God as He forms a body from the *dust of the earth* 土, and *breathing* with His *mouth* 口 into the inert "dust man's" nostrils the *breath of life* 丿 (p'ieh), Adam becomes a *living soul.* He came forth as an adult, *able to talk* 告, and also *able to walk* 辶 .

to create

土

dust

告

to speak, talk

$$土 + 口 + 丿 = 告 + 辶 = 造 \ ^5$$

dust | breath of mouth | alive | to talk | walking | to create

For the radical *walking*, there is a second form 辵 which makes the creation story even more vivid. In this pictographic representation, one can see Adam himself clearly. The three upper strokes 彡 are his *hair*; the vertical stroke | his *body*; the small horizontal stroke to the right of the vertical stroke his arm; and the remaining portions are his legs 𠃊 . The character *to create* 造 must therefore refer specifically to the creation of man and not to animals or other matter. This is even more remarkable when one understands the meaning of the Hebrew name "Adam," which is "ground." Both Hebrew and Chinese recognize Adam's origin from the dust of the earth.

辶
辵

walking

彡

hair

先

first

Adam was the first man in earth's history. The word *first* 先[6] records this fact as the most important *first* of all. Adam is recognized as a *live,* 丿 , *dust,* 土 *man* 儿. It would seem that this very primitive character for *first* would not be so constructed unless the inventor of the written language was familiar with the creation story!

The key for *fire* is 火. Here is portrayed a *man* 人 with flames radiating from him 火. Why should a *man* 人 be used as a base for *fire* unless the first man truly gave the appearance of being on fire? From this radical, *fire* 火, an enlightening discovery concerning Adam's original appearance can be made. One can learn how his body must have been clothed with a glorious shining light before sin caused the loss of his perfect character (glory) and resulted in his nakedness. (See Genesis 2:25; 3:7).

火
fire

This concept is further supported by the radical *light* 光, which again shows rays ⺌ emerging from a *first — man* 儿. In the ancient forms of writing, this is very clearly a *man* 𠔼 with *fire* 火 arising from him 光. Consequently, two different radicals for *man*, 人 and 儿, are used to represent *fire* 火 and *light* 光, both descriptive of the robe of glory. The apostle Paul in the New Testament wrote, "… man is the image of God, and the mirror of His glory" (1 Corinthians 11:7, NEB). Further, Psalm 104:1, 2 gives a description of God: "Thou art clothed with honor and majesty. Who *coverest Thyself with light as with a garment.*"[7]

火
人
man

光
light

Adam therefore resembled God in his glorious appearance, as well as being like God in his sinless character, having been made "in the image of God" (Genesis 1:26). The previously met radical for *God*, 礻, is found in the character for *ancestor* 祖. The second portion of the word, 且, means *also or moreover*. Adam,

祖
ancestor

且
also

our common *ancestor*, looked like *God*, or as *God also*. Other definitions for 祖 which further substantiate that the "ancestor" must have been Adam, are *a founder or originator, beginning, a prototype*.

Genesis tells of man's first home, "And the Lord God planted a garden in Eden, in the east; and there he put the man whom he had formed" (Genesis 2:8). This action of placing the *first* — *man* 儿 alone in the garden *enclosure* 囗 , can be seen in the character for *west* 西. It must have been the afternoon of the sixth day of creation by this time, as indicated by the position of the sun.

west

$$ 一 \;+\; 儿 \;+\; 囗 \;=\; 西^8 $$

first, one   man   enclosure   west

enclosure

The radical 田 , *landed property*, *garden*, used to represent the Garden of Eden in the several interpretations, actually looks more like an irrigated rice field than a garden. However, there are very interesting things that can be learned about the Garden from this primitive. We are told that in the center of the Garden were two special trees, the tree of life, and the tree of the knowledge of good and evil. The Garden was the meeting place of God with man. This radical is used as one component in a number of key characters which will follow in the next few chapters. The great importance of this root word will be appreciated as the book concludes.

garden, landed property

After God had placed Adam in the Garden of Eden, imagine how delighted the man must have been to discover himself in such beautiful surroundings—all about him were fragrant flowers of every hue, luxurious plants, ferns, and stately trees! No doubt there was also a placid,

43

福

happiness,
blessing

clear lake, fed by a river, to mirror the idyllic scene. Again the venerable inventor of the written language chose a meaningful ideogram for *happiness* or *blessing* 福. One can recognize every part of this character: *God* 礻 ; *one, or first* 一 ; *mouth,* representing a *person* 口 ; and *garden* 田. "God — first — person — garden" translated, indicated what "happiness is" 福[9] for Adam, the first man, a gift from God of this lovely garden home.

The busy creation week had nearly ended, except for possibly the most meaningful act of all in the greatest drama of the ages!

44

Chapter 5: They Shall Be One Flesh

How could the creation of the woman be even more spectacular than that of the man! The Biblical story relates that at first Adam was pleasantly occupied naming all the beasts, cattle, and birds which God had created, and in doing so doubtlessly noticed that all the animals were in pairs, male and female. He realized that he himself had no mate with whom to communicate and share his joys of discovery. "The man gave names to all cattle, and to the birds of the air, and to every beast of the field; but for the man there was not found a helper fit for him" (Genesis 2:20).

west

It was now late in the afternoon of this first eventful sixth day, as the sun was beginning to slip down into the western sky. The word *west* 西 pictures Adam, the *first — man* 儿, in the Garden of Eden, *an enclosure* 口 , still alone.

enclosure

$$ 一 \;+\; 儿 \;+\; 口 \;=\; 西 $$
one   man   enclosure   west

woman

Using this radical *west*, together with the primitive for *woman* 女, a new character is formed 要, meaning *to want, important, necessary, to desire, a must.* How

important, to want, necessary

true this was for Adam who felt lonely and *wanted* a "helper fit for him." A fitting mate was not only *important*, but a *necessity*! This character tells not only *what* was important and necessary for the first man (a woman) but also *when* he began to feel his need (late in the day).

$$一 + 儿 + 囗 = 西 + 女 = 要^1$$

first   man enclosure west   woman necessity

When Adam felt his need of companionship, God was ready to satisfy it. "So the Lord God caused a deep sleep to fall upon the man, and while he slept took one of his ribs and closed up its place with flesh"(Genesis 2:21).

flesh

The Chinese character for *flesh* 肉 is like a moving picture of this very operation. It consists of a *border* 冂, which could pictographically represent a surgical incision, or "flap," to be repositioned at the conclusion of the procedure. The radical *to enter or go inside* 入 appears to be halfway entering through the incision, as if God's hand were going inside Adam's chest in order to remove the woman, here pictured as another *person* 人.

border

The Genesis record continues: "And the rib which the Lord God had taken from the man he made into a woman and brought her to the man. Then the man said, 'This at last is bone of my bones and *flesh of my flesh*; she shall be called Woman, because *she was taken out of Man*'" (Genesis 2:22, 23). The *person* 人 that was taken out of Adam, molded from his rib, was Eve. How happy he was that she was actually his flesh, a part of him!

入

to enter

$$冂 + 入 + 人 = 肉$$

border to enter man   flesh
(person)

46

Even today the Chinese man refers to his wife as "my inside man." One character sometimes used for *wife* is 內,[2] which also carries the more common meaning of *within, inside, or inner,* and is very similar to the larger character for flesh 肉 . This combination of symbols for *flesh, wife* and *within, inside, inner,* seems more than coincidental when compared with the Biblical narrative of the creation of Eve, Adam's mate.

wife, inside

Thus Eve is depicted as originating in Adam. Paul in the New Testament also says this about the woman: "He [a man] is the image and glory of God; but woman is the glory of man. *For man was not made from woman, but woman from man*" (1 Corinthians 11:7, 8). Think of the uniqueness of this situation: a woman being formed from the body of a man. It happened only once!

We look to this first couple, Adam and Eve, as our common ancestors; "And God blessed them, and God said to them, 'Be fruitful and multiply, and fill the earth and subdue it' " (Genesis 1:28). The thought-provoking question might be asked: why did God not simultaneously create 10 couples, or 100, or 1,000, is order to populate the earth quickly? Why this time-consuming process with only two persons? Another alternative, God might have given the first man several wives for the same purpose. However, it was God's plan to create only one couple, male and female, for the beginning of the human family.

Of the several words in the Chinese language signifying the *beginning,* there are three characters that appear to correspond to the Genesis narrative and commemorate the most momentous *beginnings* in original history. The first of these memorializes the *beginning* of mankind,

元 *beginning, first*

二 *two*

安 *peace, tranquility*

宀 *roof*

宮 *palace*

吕 *pair*

palace (ancient form)

肉 *flesh*

元. It is composed of two familiar radicals: *two* 二 and *man* 儿, an adult. The beginning of the human family had just two individuals, also adults. The Chinese, who were often polygamous in practice, might have thought in terms of three, four, five, or ten persons (三儿, 四儿, 五儿, or 十儿) for the *beginning* of mankind. But they did not do this. The character 元 further confirms the Hebrew writings as recorded in the book of beginnings.

Adam had great *blessing and happiness* 福 with God's gift of his beautiful home in Eden (see page 44), but yet another dimension to his joy was added when he first led Eve to this idyllic abode among the flower-covered bowers. His life was now complete with a totally meaningful existence, and he was filled with *peace and tranquility* 安. This word representation shows a *roof* 宀 over a *woman* 女, implying that when the *woman* came under his *roof*, there was *peace* for both. They came and went together, knowing satisfaction and *tranquility* in each other's companionship.

Moreover, their home was a *palace* 宮, fit for the first lords of the earth, as they had been given this dominion by God. Again the *roof* 宀 is noted, with the first human *pair* 吕 as occupants. The closing scene in the drama of creation on the sixth day of this first memorable week was heralded with the institution of the marriage of Adam and Eve. The ceremony is beautifully depicted in three more primitive forms of this same character: , , and , where  and  represent a *pair* 吕;  is *flesh* 肉; and , , and 人 are three "styles" of *roof*. This is an exact pictorial representation of Genesis 2:24: "Therefore a man . . . cleaves to his wife, and they become one flesh."

The beauty of the newly created earth is beyond our imagination, but by examining the radical, *gold* 金, we can begin to appreciate the lovely domain of Adam and Eve. The three horizontal lines again suggest the realms of heaven, sea, and earth given to the first representatives of *mankind* 人. The figure 王 means *king*. The two diagonal strokes projecting from the ground 丷 remind us of the *light* 光 shining from their glorious bodies. Perhaps the ground reflected this light on scattered *golden* nuggets. There may have been other precious jewels as well, for God had created an exquisite paradise for them. "And the gold of that land is good; bdellium and onyx stone are there"[3] (Genesis 2:12).

gold

God at this point in time had finished His work of creation. "Thus the heavens and the earth were finished, and all the host of them" (Genesis 2:1). One word for *finish or complete* is 完. Again the key for *roof or house* 宀 is seen, together with 元 *beginning or first*. As previously dissected, 元 indicates two adult persons. With the foundation of this first home, therefore, the human family was begun, and the purpose of creation had been *completed*, and thus memorialized in the first marriage. Everything upon the earth had been formed for the ultimate joy and benefit of its human occupants.

完
complete,
finish

二 + 儿 = 元 + 宀 = 完
two   person first   home complete

It is significant also that this symbol 完 indicates a *finished* creation rather than a continuous process which would have large numbers of humans gradually developing from lower forms of life.

It is conceivable that 元 might be interpreted as the *beginning* of mankind from two human beings, a male and female, without reference to the Biblical story. However, the character 完 makes no sense as *completion or finish*, outside of the Genesis interpretation, for how would having a *home, roof* 宀 be the *completion* of the *beginning*? "So God created man in His own image; in the image of God He created him; *male and female* He created them. . . . On the sixth day God *completed* all the work He had been doing, and on the seventh day He ceased from all His work" (Genesis 1:27; 2:2 NEB).

to come

It is noteworthy that various primitive verbs of action depict two persons, not one or several. The reason seems to be that in the beginning there were just two people to come and go. The verb *to come* 來[4] pictures *two persons* 人人 coming from behind *a tree* 木, which has been spread apart a little to accomodate their figures. Observe also the hook, possibly representing a foot, on the vertical stroke of *to come* 來 to indicate movement. The same two people are seen *sitting* 坐 on the *ground* 土.

tree

to sit

go

The word for *go* is 往. The left radical 彳 could well be an abbreviation for *two persons*, since 亻 is a second form of *man* 人. An additional stroke 彳 could indicate *two men* instead of "a step to the left," as usually interpreted. This is indeed borne out by the ancient writing which shows the upper stroke to be an abbreviated second smaller person 𣥂 . The second portion of the word, 主, means *owner or lord*. God had given to Adam and Eve "*dominion* over the fish of the *sea* and over the birds of the *air*, and over every living thing that moves

owner, lord

upon the *earth*" (Genesis 1 : 28). The horizontal strokes in three positions picture their dominion of *heaven, sea, and earth;* the small, slanted, mark *(point)* ` at the top indicates an "anointing and authorization." The two of them were the *lords* of the earth who *went* about in each other's company, 往.[5]

Wherever Adam went, his companion *followed* 從[6] as they went about their daily activities. Here one recognizes 彳 *two persons* repeated with 从 . In order to clearly show the action of *following,* it would seem that the *two persons* 彳 must be repeated 从 , one after another, otherwise 从 could be simply interpreted as two persons. The feet are represented by the radical 止 , an abbreviation from *foot* 足. The *person* in 足 is substituted by *two persons* 从 .

In the word *all, the whole,* 僉,[7] it is documented that the whole of mankind consisted of just *two people* 人人 with *two mouths* 口 口 , surmounted by 亼 , indicating *together.*

As described in the previous chapter, Adam had the appearance of being robed in a glorious light, being made in the image and perfect character of God. Genesis notes, "And the man and his wife were both naked, and were not ashamed" (Genesis 2:25). These robes of light explain why, though naked, Adam and Eve were "not ashamed" to appear in the presence of God! A most interesting primitive radical meaning *naked, bare, or red (the color of fire)* 赤, completely confirms our supposition. This reveals a *dust* 土 , *man* 小 ; however, there are "flames" jutting out from him. Research into the ancient forms clarifies the radical, for we find a *fire* 火

to follow

foot

*all,
the whole*

*together,
collection*

*naked,
bare, red*

contained in it 赤. Several other stylized pictographs actually show two fires, portraying both Adam and Eve clothed with fire, covering their "*earthiness*" 土, as .

naked (ancient form)

Eve as well as Adam must have been clothed in light at this time, as the symbol for *glory* 榮 portrays this first sinless pair. The top radical *fire* 火 (see page 42) appears this time in duplicate and pictures *two persons* 人人 who look like fires with a bright and shining appearance. The light from them *covered* 冖 a *tree* 木. This tree very likely represented the tree of life to which Adam and Eve in their sinless and glorified state had access. As long as they ate of it, they would remain immortal, and not be subject to death. When they sinned, they became "naked" and also lost access to the tree of life. Consequently the tree in this character is very significant.

榮

glory

Conversation originated with Adam and Eve, the first two glorified humans in their perfect state of innocence. *To converse or chat* 談 shows them as fiery beings 火火 exchanging *words* 言.

談

to converse, chat

言

words

The character *ancestor* 祖, previously introduced, would appear to refer not only to Adam whom "God created in His own image," and was therefore as *God* 礻 *also* 且, but also to Eve. "In the image of God created He him; male and female created He them" (Genesis 1:27). The radical 且 takes many shapes in the ancient script, such as  or , and could even be used independently to mean *ancestor*. The horizontal lines are best explained in , which can be interpreted as *two* 二 *persons* 人.

ancestor (ancient writing)

In the first chapter it was emphasized that our planet earth has seen two very different worlds. The first, of which we have no personal acquaintance, was exquisite and perfect in its newly created state. The first man and woman were given dominion or lordship over the entire creation. It was not only from them that the earth was to be populated but also because of them that sin was introduced to our world. Therefore the original people inhabiting our globe recognized the peculiar status of this first couple, Adam and Eve.

A unique finding in the Chinese characters appears to recognize the position of our first parents and identifies the primeval world and events of that era with them. There are a number of radicals, mostly used in duplicate, which designate or have reference to *two people*. Already these have been encountered:

1. 二, used in 元 or 且.

2. 人人 , with modifications of 火火 and 彳.

3. 口口, also written as 呂.

At this point, take a moment to review the words studied in this chapter, and you will be amazed at the number of these characters containing *two people: beginning* 元 ; *ancestor* 祖 ; *to go* 往 ; *to come* 來 ; *to sit* 坐 ; *to follow* 從 ; *all* 僉 ; *glory* 榮 ; *palace* 宮 ; *to converse* 談 .

It is notable that *to go* 往, *to come* 來, and *to sit* 坐 could all be accomplished just as easily with a single person. There is no logical reason for these words to specify *two persons* 彳 , 人人 , unless they have reference to the first human couple as the subject of these verbs.

In a summarization of the creation story, observe the evolution of the following two words and how they are built upon the radicals *dust* 土 and *breath* 口 , which show God's activity in speaking things into existence, "And *God said*, 'Let the *earth bring forth* living creatures according to their kinds' "(Genesis 1 : 24). Hence, 吉 could be an abbreviated form to represent the "product of creation," and used thus in other figures. For God had commanded, by a word from His *mouth* 口 , the *earth* 土 to bring forth plants and animals. When everything was in readiness for man, He *created* 造 Adam also from the dust. (See page 41)

garden

perfect,
benevolent

Adam and Eve rejoiced in their togetherness with God in their beautiful *garden* 園 . Here is the climax of the total God-energy expended, a glorious creation 吉 with a handsome couple 伙 . Observe *two persons*, 亻 and 〈 , the second issuing from the side of the first, neatly depicting the creation of Eve from Adam's rib. This event had taken place in the Garden of Eden. The figure 伙 is reminiscent of another similar word, 仁,[8] meaning *perfect, in loving harmony*. This also depicts two people with the numeral *two* 二, also attached to the side of the first *man* 亻 . The only two *perfect* (sinless) human beings ever to exist were Adam and Eve, having the Garden as their home. An *enclosure* 口 defines the boundaries of the Garden of Eden.

enclosure

$$土 + 口 + 伙 + 口 = 園^9$$

dust   breath   two   enclosure   garden
persons

Thus ended the sixth day of earth's history. "And on the seventh day God finished His work which He had done, and He rested on the seventh day from all His work which He had done. So God blessed the seventh day and hallowed it, because on it God rested from all His work which He had done in creation" (Genesis 2:2, 3). As a memorial of God's handiwork, the weekly cycle of seven days was instituted.

The week is not an institution based on natural phenomena, such as the day when the earth turns on its axis, the month with its lunar relationship, nor the year marking the earth's excursion about the sun. The week dates exclusively to the great original days of creation, a period of time that is observed by the Chinese in spite of their thousands of years of isolation from the rest of the world and its customs.

七

seven

An old Chinese saying, *the returning seventh day*, 七日來復 points up the fact that from very early times the Chinese have recognized the recurring seven day cycle which marks the week.

Even today, the seventh day of the first lunar month of the Chinese year is known as the "birthday of mankind" 人 日, and literally means *man's* 人 *day* 日 . Just as it was not the day of man's creation which was to be celebrated, but rather the following day of rest, so the Chinese also celebrate the seventh day as a lingering memorial of God's creative work and the creation of mankind.

日

day

One cannot help but be impressed with the composition of these ideograms which demonstrate so vividly the ancient history of earth's beginnings, heretofore documented only by the Hebrew writings. But this identical story has also been locked into the written Chinese language and preserved for more than 4,000 years for our investigation and study.

Chapter 6 : The Fruit Tragedy

"How can you portray the word *temptation* by using just four words?" asked the quiz master on a popular television program. "I will give you a hint by supplying one of the four words. Now listen carefully — the word is *garden*." Immediately one of the contestants had the answer: "Garden ... Eve ... serpent ... apple!"

"That is correct!" responded the questioner. And who would not have equated "temptation" with the episode recorded in Genesis? Many and varied have been the cartoons created through the years which depict a hapless Eve who stands coveting a delectable piece of fruit held out by the serpentine tempter.

How does the most ancient of all picture-writers (for it would be inappropriate to call him a cartoonist) illustrate the word *to covet or desire*? Is it mere happenstance that *to covet* 婪 utilizes two *trees* 林 and a *woman* 女 ? The Biblical record says, "So when the *woman* saw that the *tree* was good for food, and that it was a delight to the eyes, and that the tree was to be *desired* to make one wise, she took of its fruit and ate" (Genesis 3:6). It was the woman, Eve, and not the man who first desired

to covet, desire

the fruit of the forbidden tree, and succumbed to the temptation to eat it.

$$ 林 \; + \; 女 \; = \; 婪 $$

trees   *woman*   *desire, covet*

But why two trees instead of one?

As the Genesis narrative is recalled, one discovers that there were two important trees specified in the Garden. "The Lord God planted a garden in Eden, in the east; and there He put the man whom He had formed. And out of the ground the Lord God made to grow every tree that is pleasant to the sight and good for food, the *tree of life* also in the midst of the garden, and the *tree of the knowledge of good and evil*" (Genesis 2:8, 9). These two noteworthy trees were found side by side in the very middle of the garden. The "tree of life" is further described in Revelation 22:2 as having "twelve kinds of fruits, yielding its fruit each month; and the leaves of the tree were for the healing of the nations." This tree had very wonderful life-giving properties, and Adam and Eve were commanded to eat of it without restriction. The second tree sounded ominous, "the tree of the knowledge of good and evil."

When God created human beings, He gave them freedom of choice and thereby risked losing them by allowing them this freedom. God had placed Adam and Eve in a luxuriant garden, lovingly providing for their every need with luscious fruits and nuts of every kind. He had forbidden only one thing: "He [the Lord God] told the man, 'You may eat from every tree in the garden, but not from the tree of the knowledge of good and evil; for on the day that you eat from it, you will certainly die' " (Genesis 2:16, 17 NEB). Actually, this was a test of loyalty to ascertain whether or not the human family would choose of their own free will to obey God, their beneficent Creator. For by disobedience, they would actually separate themselves from the Life - Giver.

The use of *two trees* 林 in a character therefore is significant and could indicate that a choice must be made between them: eating the fruit of one symbolized obedience and life, but the other, disloyalty and death.

An abbreviated character for God is 示 (see page 36). When a hook is added to the middle stroke 示, a verb is formed meaning [God] *commands or notifies.* The word *forbidden, to warn, to prohibit, or restrict* is written 禁 and pictographically records God's original commands regarding these two specific trees. One can understand then that Adam and Eve had ample instruction and warning by God. How meaningful that to this day the Chinese still write about trees when using the words *forbidden* and *covet*!

forbidden, to warn

God had an enemy, a mighty angel, who had no regard for the just laws of God. A mystery remains, hard to understand, how Lucifer had fallen from his high position as an honored angel, standing in the very presence of God, to being a renegade, an outcast. Lucifer, as a subordinate, had become jealous of God's creative power, and in aspiring to a higher state, had determined to dethrone God. "How you are fallen from heaven, O Day Star [Lucifer] . . . You said in your heart, 'I will ascend to heaven; above the stars of God I will set my throne on high; . . . I will make myself like the Most High!' " (Isaiah 14:12-14). In reference to this rebellion of Lucifer, it is recorded: "Now war arose in heaven, Michael and his angels fighting against the dragon; and the dragon and his angels fought; but they were defeated, and there was no longer any place for them in heaven. And the great dragon was thrown down, that ancient serpent, who is called the Devil and Satan, the deceiver of the whole world—he was thrown down to the earth, and his angels were thrown down with him" (Revelation 12:7-9).

Adam and Eve had been cautioned regarding this crafty foe who would attempt to align them as accomplices in his warfare against God. They had also been advised of the natural results of disobedience, which would put them into disharmony and separate them from their Creator and Life-Giver. Would they listen to Lucifer and his subtle reasoning, or believe that God was all-wise and all-loving? The choice was theirs.

to go

One might think that since there were only two people in existence, Adam and Eve would usually be in each other's company. The word *to go* 往 (see page 50), shows just this. There were *two persons* 彳 who were *lords* 主, with dominion over the whole earth. But one day as Eve had left Adam's side to pass through the middle of the garden, she suddenly heard a strange voice. It was not Adam's voice, and the sound of it arrested her, and she stopped, curious to know from whence it came. She looked with amazement into the branches of the tree of the knowledge of good and evil where a beautiful serpent rested. Was this creature also able to speak? Lucifer, in the guise of a serpent, had been waiting for just this opportunity when Eve might be alone, for the couple often passed by this tree.

Is it possible that the serpent, which allowed itself to be the medium for Lucifer, actually had wings at this time, and was able to stand upright? Such could be inferred from the Genesis story, for when God afterward cursed the creature for its part in the temptation of Eve, He said, "Because you have done this, cursed are you above all cattle, and above all wild animals; *upon your belly you shall go,* and dust you shall eat all the days of your life" (Genesis 3:4). This statement suggests that its punishment was a new crawling posture. Might it formerly have been able to fly? The Chinese primitive for *reptile* 豸 certainly supports this. One could hardly guess from the pictograph that this upright figure represents today's concept of a crawling snake!

reptile

In analyzing the word picture for *reptile* 豸, one sees a standing snakelike body 丿. Attached to the left side are three strokes 彡 which can indicate either *hair or feathers.* Neither are ordinarily considered a natural part of snake anatomy, however feathers are certainly an integral part of wings. But the word for *wings* is 羽, and one wing on the snake body could conceivably be written 彡. Some ancient forms of this radical actually suggest a pair of wings: 𦓇 or 𦒰. The reptile also appears to have two eyes ㄑ in its head. And so the Chinese depict a rather wise-looking and versatile creature!

hair, feathers

wings

There can be no doubt that the ancient Chinese had an accurate knowledge of the temptation of Eve by the devil, or Lucifer, in the agent of the serpent. The word *devil* 鬼 clearly describes her encounter with him. First of all, one recognizes that this key represents something alive or moving when seeing the "p'ieh" 丿 at the top of the radical. The *garden* 田 is noted, as well as a *man* 儿.

devil

The Fruit Tragedy

厶 secretly, privately

A new primitive 厶 indicates *privately or secretly*. Putting the story together, one sees the complete representation of the devil's seduction of the woman. He *moved* into the *Garden* in the disguise of a serpent to speak *privately* with the voice of a *man* to Eve.

丿 + 田 + 儿 + 厶 = 鬼[1]
[*motion*] garden man privately devil

It would seem that in this radical for the *devil* 鬼 the ancient Chinese had nicknamed him the "secret garden man," whereas Adam is characterized either as a "dust man" in the word *first* 先, or as a "fieryman" in the word *fire* 火.

魔 tempter, demon

广 a covering

This word *devil* 鬼 is frequently qualified in another character 魔 meaning *tempter or demon*. Note here that the devil is hidden under two *trees* 林, which specifies that site of the two special trees in the middle of the Garden of Eden. Above the trees is a *covering* 广 which records that the *devil* took refuge under the *cover* of the *trees* (and was also camouflaged with the serpent as his medium), when he *tempted* Eve.

丿 + 田 + 儿 + 厶 = 鬼 + 林 + 广 = 魔
[*motion*] garden man privately devil trees cover tempter

The devil began his conversation with Eve by posing a question, "Did God say, 'You shall not eat of any tree of the garden?'" (Genesis 3:1). As Eve answered, she probably began to wonder why God had placed the restriction. "God said, 'You shall not eat of the fruit of the tree which is in the midst of the garden, neither shall you touch it, lest you die'" (Genesis 3:3). The

62

serpent then very daringly declared to the woman, "*You will not die*, For God knows that when you eat of it your eyes will be opened, and you will be like God, knowing good and evil" (Genesis 3:4).

How bold for the devil to openly refute God's Word when he told Eve, "You will not die!" Did this mean that the devil was promising the woman immortality, whereas God said man would become mortal if he disobeyed? Lucifer was determined to prove God a liar, for God had said that if the forbidden fruit were eaten, death would result. It surely must have seemed at first that the devil's claim of immortality for mankind was true when Adam and Eve did not immediately die after eating the forbidden fruit. It was actually a number of years later that Abel, one of Adam's sons, was killed by his brother. At last many centuries later, Adam himself also died. Man was indeed subject to death! To escape from this predicament, the devil must perpetrate another theory, that actually there is a part of man that never dies, called "the soul." In the Chinese character for *soul* 魂, the source of the idea of the immortality of the soul is depicted, for the character reads, the devil *says* 云.

魂
soul

云
to say

$$ 鬼 + 云 = 魂^2 $$
devil   says   soul

It was the devil who said, "You will not die." Lucifer, with the help of this fallen angels, is able to cleverly impersonate the voice, mannerisms, and appearance of the dead by ghostly apparitions. For this reason, God has completely condemned witchcraft and spiritualistic mediums who communicate with the "departed spirits."

The warning is given in the New Testament, "Now the works of the flesh are manifest, which are these : . . . Idolatry, *witchcraft*, hatred . . . of which I tell you before, as I have also told you in time past, that they which do such things shall not inherit the kingdom of God" (Galatians 5:19-21 KJV). These "departed spirits" are actually the fallen angels (Revelation 12:9) who are attempting to demonstrate that the soul is that portion of man which never dies.

snare, net

Lucifer carefully laid his *snare* 罒 of four attractive statements, all with the intent to deceive, which beguiled Eve into disobedience:

1. "You will not die.
2. "God knows that when you eat of it your eyes will be opened.
3. "You will be like God.
4. [You will] "know good and evil" (Genesis 3:4, 5).

four

There are additional symbols, 网 and 冗, for *net*, *snare*. Interestingly, the numeral *four* 四 has similarities to each form of *snare*, for it can be compressed within a character to 罒 , and anciently it was written 𝕽 or as X . Eve's downfall was to be caught in Lucifer's *snare* of *four* deceptive statements.

beginning

"So when the woman saw that the tree was good for food, and that it was a delight to the eyes, and that the tree was to be desired to make one wise, she took of the fruit and ate" (Genesis 3:6). Commemorating this sad historical event is the character 始, a second word for *beginning*—this time evidently indicating the *beginning* of sin. The scene is of a woman, by herself, eating the forbidden fruit. It takes three elements to construct this character: the *woman* 女; *secretly, alone* 厶 ; and to indicate *eating*, a *mouth* 口. Two ancient renderings of this character especially support the interpretation: 𡥜 shows the radical *secretly* ◊ , like a fruit, actually disappearing into the open *mouth* Ͱ of the *woman* 𦮼 . A more modified form 𡥕 depicts a *hand* 𠂤 feeding the *mouth* ▽ of the *woman* ὃ . Thus the entire episode of the genesis of sin is recorded in a single ideograph.

beginning
(ancient
form)

女	+	厶	+	口	=	始
woman		*secretly*		*mouth* (*for eating*)		*beginning* (*of sin*)

Eve next offered Adam the forbidden fruit. "She also gave some to her husband, and he ate" (Genesis 3:6). Adam, unlike Eve, was not deceived (1 Timothy 2:14). Perhaps it was because of love for his wife and his unwillingness to be separated from her that he willfully disobeyed God when he accepted and ate the fruit which Eve offered him. Our first parents sinned in accepting the words of the subtle tempter over the warning of their loving and all-wise Creator.

This whole sad story of mankind's fall into sin is preserved in the Chinese language in such explicit detail that one cannot miss the message if the eyes are opened to discern it. The Hebrews and the ancient Chinese people were in widely separated parts of the world, and yet their stories support one another. Actually, the

Chinese characters containing this record preceded the Genesis writings by many centuries. The striking similarities in the Hebrew annals and the Chinese calligraphy will become more and more apparent as the Genesis chronicle unfolds.

Chapter 7 : Dust to Dust

In the beginning, man's original character was virtous, 人之初性本善. This ancient classical nursery rhyme can be recited with sing-song lilt by nearly every Chinese child. It carries a proverbial truth. Unfortunately, man's perfect sinless character was lost by a single willful act. Adam ate the forbidden fruit that his wife offered him, knowing full well that he was disobeying the express command of his Creator; and he was perhaps for the moment ignoring the ultimate result.

Immediately a change came over them. "Then the *eyes of both were opened,* and they knew that they were *naked*; and they sewed fig leaves together and made themselves aprons" (Genesis 3:7). Adam and Eve had been created in the image of God, and in their sinless, perfect state had been clothed with a glorious light, appearing as though on fire with *glory* 榮 (see pages 42 and 52). This glory, symbolizing their sinless characters, mirroring that of God, began to fade after they had chosen to disobey God's direct command. Their "eyes were opened," as Lucifer had promised, but the result was not as Eve had envisioned! Consequently, for the first

glory

time, they became aware of their nakedness and, full of shame, felt their need of a covering. They took what was close at hand and made for themselves "aprons" of large fig leaves to hide their nakedness.

naked

There are three characters which indicate *naked*: 倮, 躶, and 裸.[1] It will be immediately observed that the second element 果 in each is identical, and this, interestingly enough, means *fruit* (from *garden* 田 and *tree* 木)! The first portion of two characters has to do with the person: one is *man* 亻; and the second, the *body* 身, indicating what is to be covered. The third character contains the radical 衤 which means *clothing*. Thus all three characters correlate with the Genesis story regarding the contrived covering for the nakedness of Adam and Eve.

fruit

Why should the symbol for *fruit* 果 be used instead of one for "leaves"? In Genesis, the leaves of the fig tree are specified as being selected to make the "aprons." Of all the large-leafed trees in the garden, it is noteworthy that the leaves of a *fruit* tree were used for the garments. Thus three fruit trees are actually mentioned in Genesis; they are of prime importance to the story of the fall of Adam and Eve. They ate of the *fruit* of the forbidden tree; they thereby lost access to the *fruit* of the tree of life; and they used the leaves of the *fig* tree to cover their nakedness. Is it not appropriate then to single out *fruit*, rather than leaves, since all trees have leaves but not fruit?

body

衣

clothing

It was God's custom to visit in face-to-face communion with Adam and Eve each day in the garden. The time was approaching when He would appear. "And they heard the sound of the Lord God walking in the garden in the cool of the day" (Genesis 3:8). The purpose of *God's* 示 daily visit with Adam and Eve is substantiated by the word 視, meaning *to inspect*. A new radical, *eye* 目, is noted and combined with 儿. 見, *to observe, see, visit, interview, or meet* is thereby further expressed.

視
to inspect

目
eye

Ordinarily when God came to visit with Adam and Eve, it was the highlight of the entire day, but on this occasion, after their glorious covering had faded, they were afraid and attempted to hide. "And they heard the sound of the Lord God walking in the garden in the cool of the day, and the man and his wife *hid themselves* from the presence of the Lord God *among the trees* of the garden" (Genesis 3:8). The word *to hide* 躱 is composed of three elements, two of which have been previously studied: *body* 身 and tree 木. The figure 乃 in this instance means *is*, so that literally this character is saying *the body is a tree*, or Adam and his wife are trees. As they hid among the trees, they were not seen, only the trees.

見
*to see,
to visit*

躱
to hide

乃
is

來
to come

身 + 乃 + 木 = 躱
body   is   tree   to hide

"But the Lord God called to the man, and said to him, 'Where are you?' And he said, 'I heard the sound of Thee in the garden, and I was afraid, because I was naked, and I hid myself'" (Genesis 3:9,10). At this point, they came forth from among the trees. The word *to come* 來 shows this exactly. The *tree* radical 木 has been stretched out a bit to accomodate *two persons* 人人. At the base of the *tree* is also a hook, or foot 來, which gives the word action, *to come* (from behind a tree).

Having presented themselves before the Lord, Adam

69

and Eve were filled with remorse as they awaited God's next words: "Who told you that you were naked? Have you eaten of the tree of which I commanded you not to eat?" (Genesis 3:11). As a verdict was reached and the consequences specified, God said to the woman, "I will greatly multiply your *pain* [*sorrow*, KJV] in childbearing; in *pain* you shall bring forth children, yet your desire shall be for your husband, and he shall rule over you" (Genesis 3:16).

sorrow, pain

Sorrow, distress, or pain is written with two characters, 苦楚. Note first the second of these 楚 which again depicts the two trees. The lower portion of figure denotes *a piece* 疋 , and in this case might refer to the forbidden *piece* of fruit which Eve took from the tree, thereby bringing sorrow upon the first couple and in turn upon the whole human race. Depicted in this figure is a single *person*: ∧ indicates the legs; ⼘ shows the body with the right arm; and at the top of the representation ⺪ is the left arm with hand in hooked position, as if taking something. Does this picture Eve in the very act of stealing the forbidden *piece* of fruit 疋 ?

a piece

The ancient ideographs verify the assertion: a *piece* may be represented as ⵡ or ⵣ . Again the left arm is reaching out for something. 楚 furthermore has been stylized in one form as 㸚. The *trees* 林 here enclose a *person* ⼂ , but note the *hand* ⼃ on the person which is the center of interest. Eve's act of disobedience is thus clearly depicted, and the reason for her *sorrow and pain* becomes apparent.

苦

sorrow, bitter, suffering

The second word for *sorrow, suffering, bitter* is 苦, which literally translates *ancient* 古, *grass, herbs, weeds* 艹 . This character, perhaps, was intended to memorialize Adam's sorrow, for God declared to him, "Because you have listened to the voice of your wife, and have eaten of the tree of which I commanded you, 'You shall not eat of it,' cursed is the ground because of you; in toil [*sorrow*, KJV] you shall eat of it all the days of your life; *thorns and thistles* it shall bring forth to you; and you *shall eat the plants of the field*. In the sweat of your face you shall eat bread till you return to the ground, for out of it you were taken; you are dust, and to dust you shall return' "(Genesis 3:17-19).

古
ancient

From this *ancient* 古 time forward, man has had to work hard to secure provisions from the earth in the form of *plants* of the field 艹 to sustain life. The figure 古 also might be pictographically interpreted as illustrating eating, using the *ten* 十 fingers to put food into the *mouth* 口.

艹
grass, weeds, plants

十	+	口	=	古	+	艹	=	苦 [2]
ten [*fingers*]		*mouth*		*ancient*		*plants, weeds*		*sorrow, bitter*

The food also was not as delicious as before, as some plants were *bitter* to the taste. Thus when the two characters 苦 楚 are written together, as they often are, to designate sorrow, one sees depicted the *sorrow* of both Adam and Eve.

God, the loving Creator, knew man's frame, his weaknesses, his bent to sin since Lucifer had filled his mind with unholy desires. Therefore the restrictions and apparent punishments that were placed on Adam and Eve were to be blessings typical of God's long-range, eternal love-disciplines to help remold their injured characters. God also advised them of the death process. The warning, "You will die," is better translated, "dying,

71

thou shalt die." Death was not necessarily a visible terminal cessation of life but a gradual deterioration and degenerative process which would affect many aspects of life. For Eve, and all womankind, the change would somehow affect the bearing of children, which doubtless God had originally planned to be a totally joyful experience. By Eve's disobedience, her original status as an equal with her husband would be changed; in general, women through the succeeding generations have suffered an inferior consideration.

刑
to punish

干
to offend

So God pronounced the penalty coming upon the first man and woman as an inevitable result which they had brought upon themselves. The word *to punish* 刑 shows that *two people* were involved and that there were *two offenses*. The radical for *offend* 干 is doubled 卄 in order to show that there were two indicted. 刂 is a *knife*, suggesting the serious type of punishment.

卄   +   刂   =   刑

to offend   *knife*   *to punish*
(doubled)

united,
together

A similar character 幷 meaning *united, together,* and indicating their partnership in rebellion, appears to have the same origin. Note that the *points* ʻʻ of "anointing" in the ancient writing for this symbol 𢆶, represent *two persons* 〉〉 who are *offenders* 卄. Ancient ideograms for *to punish* 刑 are similar: 㓝, where 丿 pictures a *knife* 刂. One venerable calligrapher was even more explicit: 㓹, adding *dust* 土, which portrays the ultimate fate of the offenders as well!

The type of *punishment* indicated by 刑 is corporal, and in the case of Adam meant daily hard toil, and for

Eve pain in childbirth, with death as the ultimate result
of transgression for both.

Another character meaning *to fine or punish* 罰
portrays the basic cause of the whole problem. Note
that 罒 , meaning *snare or four* (see page 64) is further
qualified by the key, *words, speech, statement* 言. The
pictograph once more indicates that it was the "net of
words" or *four statements* uttered by the serpent and
believed by Adam and Eve which resulted in their great
loss. Note also the *four* lines issuing from the mouth in
言.

罒 net (four) + 言 statement + 刂 knife = 罰 to fine [3]

This character for *fining* 罰 refers to the confiscation
of property or means. For Adam and Eve, the penalty
meant not only a loss of their Eden home but also their
dominion as lords of the entire earth. The two characters
together 刑 罰 represent *punishment* in the Chinese and
exactly agrees with the Genesis account when the sentence pronounced upon the hapless pair involved loss
of both life and dominion or *lordship* 主 over heaven,
earth, and seas. They ended up being *workers* 工, as
one of the horizontal lines representing their three-fold
dominion is removed. The "appointment" ヽ at the
top of the figure is also withdrawn.

God had said to Adam, " 'Cursed is the ground because of you, . . . *thorns and thistles* it shall bring forth
to you' " (Genesis 3:17, 18). Implements have been used
through the ages, and more recently, machines have
been invented and various chemical poisons produced
in an attempt to destroy the ever-present and unwanted

罰 *to fine, punish*

罒 *net (four)*

言 *words, statement*

主 *lord*

weeds that thrive and thwart man's agricultural efforts. Mankind has certainly been punished by these noxious plants through all time, but the world as a whole little realizes that "thorns and thistles" were placed on the earth as a "curse." It appears that the venerable Chinese recognized them as a form of punishment to the human family.

thorns

grass

刑

punishment

There are two characters for *thorns or brambles*, 棘 and 荆 , which tell the Genesis story. The character 荆 has two parts. *Grass, weeds, or plant life is* 艹 , and it will be remembered that this radical was first encountered in the word *sorrow* 苦, in reference to Adam's punishment (see page 70). The remaining portion of the character will be recognized as *punishment* 刑 . The Chinese hereby record *weeds, plants* 艹 as a *punishment* 刑 , and *thorns* 荆 were seen as a curse for man's transgression.

开 + 刂 = 刑 + 艹 = 荆
offender (doubled)   *knife*   *punishment*   *weeds*   *thorns*

Actually, they were a form of discipline (and indirectly even a blessing), to keep sinful man from idleness, which would only tend to increase the opportunity for wickedness. God's concern for man's welfare is revealed when He said, " 'Cursed is the ground for *thy* sake' " (Genesis 3:17 KJV).

棘

thorns

The second character for *thorns, troublesome* 棘 , depicts the familiar two *trees* 林 reminiscent of the Garden of Eden. Only now the trees are no longer accessible, for as God expelled man from Eden, "at the east of the garden of Eden he' placed the cherubim, and a flaming sword which turned every way, to guard the way to the tree of life" (Genesis 3:24). On each of the *trees* 林 is a *border* 冂 , or fence. Adam and Eve are kept away from the two trees in the Garden. This character 棘 for *thorns* is a reminder of the punishment and exclusion from Eden.

Man was demoted from lord to laborer by the dismal sentence: "In the sweat of your face you shall eat bread till you return to the *ground*, for out of it you were taken; you are *dust*, and to *dust* you shall return" (Genesis 3:19). The ultimate fate was death and the *tomb* 塋 .

tomb, grave

$$火火 + 冖 + 土 = 塋$$

火火	冖	土	塋
fires	cover	dust	tomb
(two persons)			

glory

It is enlightening to compare the two characters *glory* 榮 and *grave* 塋 . The former has the *tree* (of life) 木 and represents immortal life, which was God's original intention when mankind was given the tree of life. This, however, has been replaced by *dust* 土 in the second figure, indicating that Adam became mortal and subject to death and the grave.

Happily, the character for *grave* 塋 also carries a promise of future *glory* to all who return to dust believing in the saving blood of Jesus Christ. Paul states: "Just as we have borne the image of the man of dust [Adam], we shall also bear the image of the man of Heaven [Christ]" (1 Corinthians 15:49). That image is His glory— His perfect character, as explained in Romans 8:29,30 : "For those whom He foreknew He also predestined to be conformed to the *image of His Son*, . . . And those whom He predestined He also called; and those whom He called He also justified; and those whom He justified He also *glorified*."

God did not mete out justice without mercy, for He looked upon the man and woman whom He had created and, with great love and concern, provided for them new garments, symbolizing the hope of salvation from their fallen state. "And the Lord God made for Adam and for his wife garments of skins and clothed them" (Genesis 3:21). This meant the taking of animals' lives for the first time as God made garments of the skins, symbolic of the future death of His own Son, the Lamb of God, as the world's Savior. Their improvised aprons of fig leaves were replaced, and they had a new *appearance or form* 形. The *offenders* (doubled) 开 were covered by woolly *(hairy)* 彡 garments. An ancient sheep radical also demonstrates this "woolly" appearance 羊 .

appearance, form

$$ 开 \quad + \quad 彡 \quad = \quad 形 $$

offenders (two)   hair   form, appearance

The radical for *clothing* 衣 likewise shows that God provided a *covering* 亠 for the guilty pair 化 (recall the discussion of *garden* 園 on page 60, which portrays a *man* 亻 with a second *person* 匕 issuing from his side). This is seen even more clearly in the older calligraphy as 𠄏 , 𠔉 , or 𠆢 . The *two persons* are depicted as 化 , 川 , or 𠃊 .

clothing

It was thus that death came into God's perfect creation—as a result of Adam's sin. The lesson which God intended to teach through the sacrificial act was to demonstrate that sin is costly, for only by death of the sinless Son of God, Jesus, could the full penalty be met. God Himself provided a way of escape to the repentant ones who had faith in His vicarious sacrifice for man.

This is further demonstrated by the third word for *beginning* 初,which pictures *clothing* 衣 and a *knife* 刀,

beginning

indicating that only death by slaying a symbolic innocent animal could provide clothing. The third historic *beginning* 初 denotes the initiation of God's plan of redemption and grace for the human race. Note these earlier forms which completely confirm the Genesis narrative: 𝄞 where 廿 depicts *two* ⌒ *mouths* (persons) 廿 being *covered*, ⌒ and a *knife* 刀 . Observe a variation of style of writing in 𝄞 , again portraying the same!

刀
リ
knife

The original exchange of garments becomes the oft repeated symbolism later in the Bible for the imputed and imparted righteousness of Christ on the sinner's behalf. The same participants as in the Eden drama are portrayed by Zechariah 3:1-4: "Then He showed me Joshua the high priest [Adam, sinner] standing before the Angel of the Lord [the Lord God, Christ] and Satan [the serpent, Lucifer] standing at his right hand to accuse him. And the Lord said to Satan, 'The Lord rebuke you, O Satan! The Lord who has chosen Jerusalem [God's people] rebuke you! Is not this a brand [sinner] plucked from the fire? Now Joshua was standing before the Angel, clothed with filthy garments [fig leaves, self-righteousness]. And the Angel said to those who were standing before Him, 'Remove the filthy garments from him.' And to him He said, 'Behold, I have taken your iniquity away from you, and I will clothe you with rich apparel'" [garments of skins which God provided, symbolizing the righteous character of the Lamb of God].

The world's first tragedy ended when Adam and Eve were expelled from their beautiful Garden home in Eden. "Therefore the Lord God sent him forth from the Garden of Eden, to till the ground from which he was taken. He drove out the man" (Genesis 3:23, 24). Adam was sent out of the Garden, no more to enjoy its bountiful fruits. The ground had been cursed, and from that time on he must toil vigorously to destroy unwanted weeds in order to produce food from the soil for his family.

Adam was driven out of the Garden because God did not want him to become an immortal sinner with access to the tree of life, thus perpetuating his life as long as he ate of its fruit. " 'Lest he [the man] put forth his hand and take also of the tree of life, and eat, and live forever' — therefore the Lord God sent him forth from the garden of Eden" (Genesis 3:22, 23).

to drive out,
to expel

offender

to go,
travel

foot

to move one's
abode

The word to *drive out, expel* 赶 is an interesting combination. In it is recognized an *offender* 干. Because Adam had become an offender, God told them that they must *go, or travel* 走. A closer examination of this radical reveals an abbreviated form 止 of the radical for *foot* 足. Substituting for the *person* 口 at the top of this figure are actually *two* 二 *persons* superimposed upon 丨 as 丰. An ancient form 豆 verifies that *two persons* originally *went*. Instead of writing the two figures separately, the character is written without lifting the writing instrument, and simplified to 走. Combining the various portions, the word *to drive out or expel* 赶 is formed. This contains the reason for the expulsion: *two people* had become *offenders*.

$$干 \; + \; 走 \; = \; 赶$$

offender   *to go*   *to expel*
(2 persons)

Under the death sentence, Adam and Eve left their lovely garden home *to move their abode* 徙. The older writing of this character reveals exciting details not seen

78

in the more recent "shorthand" edition. illustrates the *two persons* 彳 ; a *roof* 宀 ; *two fires* 炎 , representing Adam and Eve in their glorious state; *dust* 土 , indicative of their newly declared mortality; and *walking* 辶 . This figure reiterates the same idea as seen in *tomb* 塋 .

to move one's abode (ancient writing)

Recall once again that the character for *Garden* 園 shows *two people* 夫 , (亻 and <) in an *enclosure* 囗 . After being expelled from the Garden, Adam and Eve must have gone some distance, for the character depicting *distant* 遠 reveals not only the loss of the Garden enclosure 囗 , but also shows them *walking* 辶 .

garden

Furthermore, 遠 may mean *to alienate or deviate.* Certainly the willful disobedience with the resultant expulsion from their Garden home caused a feeling of alienation from the Creator. This had already been demonstrated by their attempt to hide.   A familiar saying of Confucius still expresses the fear of close communion with God, for this philosopher advised, "Respect God, but keep your distance."

enclosure

The word *robe* 袁 [4] also contains the same cluster of radicals as seen in *garden* 園 and *distant* 遠 and is reminiscent of Adam and Eve's receiving their garments from God at the time of their banishment from the Garden of Eden.

distant, alienate, deviate

So that the exiled pair could not return to the Garden, "at the east of the garden of Eden He placed the cherubim, and *a flaming sword* which turned every way, to guard the way to the tree of life" (Genesis 3:24). The character in Chinese for a *double-edged sword* is 劍 . Analysis of this proves to be a fascinating study. In this a *knife* 刂 (also 刀) is seen.   The complete figure 僉

robe

double edged sword

刀
刂
knife

僉
all, the whole

灬
fire

indicates *all, the whole.* Looking at it closely, it is formed of three elements: 亼, 口 口 and 人人, the latter two picturing *two persons*; it could represent Adam and Eve, who at this time comprised *all, or the whole* of mankind. The older calligraphy inscribes this figure in two significant ways:  and . In the first, the attachment of *mouth*  to a *person*  would seem to indicate *two persons having two mouths.* In the second figure the symbols for *persons* 人 人 have been replaced by the alternate radical for *fire* 灬.

If the venerable inventor of the Chinese writing were to pictographically represent the very first sword in the history of mankind, he would have to recall the story of the two-edged or *two-mouthed* 口 口, *flaming* 火 火 sword in the hand of the angel guarding the gate of Eden after Adam and Eve had been expelled. The ancient calligrapher must have greatly enjoyed putting together this symbol for *two-edged sword* 劍; for he could not only describe the original fiery weapon with its two "biting" edges but at the same time represent the unfortunate first couple by two figures: 口 口, also representing the two sharp edges of the sword; and 人 人 (modified from 火 火 because they had just lost their original glorious robes of light); yet 人 人 is still used to represent the flaming aspect as noted above in .

Man did not suffer alone in the disobedient act that separated him from God's presence. God also sorrowed and planned a remedy: "For God so loved the world that He gave His only Son, that whoever believes in Him should not perish but have eternal life" (John 3:16). The day will come when believing man will be delivered from the curse of Adam. At that time Christ will forever remove the "thorns and thistles" and, having provided the repentant sinner with a perfect robe of righteousness, will bring him once more to the renewed paradise Garden of God.

Chapter 8 : The Seed of Rebellion

At the time when Adam and Eve were expelled from the Garden of Eden, they had no children. As a result of her disobedience God told Eve that she would have sorrow and pain in childbearing. But God had also given this first pair hope with the promise of a Redeemer, for He had said to Lucifer, who had beguiled Eve in the guise of the serpent, " I will put enmity between you and the woman, and between your seed and *her Seed*; He shall bruise your head, and you shall bruise His heel" (Genesis 3:15). So despite the pain of childbearing, Adam and Eve eagerly desired a son, who they hoped would be *that Seed*, the promised Deliverer.

孕
pregnant

The first human conception is recorded in the Chinese written language as a son. The word *pregnant* 孕 is made up of two symbols, *is* 乃, and a *son* 子. This character even looks *pregnant*, with the son contained within the larger figure!

乃
is

子
son

The Genesis story relates, "Now Adam knew Eve his wife; and she conceived, and bore Cain, saying(RSV), 'I have gotten a man, the Lord' " (Genesis 4:1 AAT).[1] The name "Cain" in Hebrew means "got." They named

Cain in accordance with their hope that they had "gotten" a Savior from God. They did not realize that their first-born son was not to be the Promised One, but instead he would become the cause of further great sorrow in their lives. A second son, Abel, was born soon afterward.

As Cain and Abel grew through their youthful years, they were a source of happiness to their parents. Cain enjoyed agricultural pursuits and provided the family with a bountiful supply of fruits and vegetables. Abel, on the other hand, loved animals and kept flocks of sheep. This occupation met other needs of the family, not only supplying wool for clothing but also lamb offerings for their worship of God. The slaying of the lamb they understood was to symbolize the Deliverer, who would ultimately be slain as man's Substitute and thus remove the death penalty. Through this act of worship, they demonstrated their faith in the promised Savior, who would thereby once more restore their lost righteous characters. The children had been taught by their parents to kneel before the lamb offered on an altar.

righteousness

The word for *righteousness* 義 appears to have been derived from this original act of worship, asking forgiveness for sin. A *sheep* 羊 is found in this figure, and beneath it, 我, picturing *I, me, we* kneeling before the Lamb of God, who alone covers me and brings *righteousness*. Further dissection of this last character for *me* reveals a composite of hand 手 and a lance or *spearhead* 戈. This specifies that the slaying of the lamb is by *me*, by my own *hand*, using a *spearhead*, indicating that my sins would bring death to the innocent Lamb of God. This interpretation is verified by ancient forms for *me* 羕 and *righteousness* 羕, both of which portray a *hand* 㐅 and *spear* 㦮.

sheep

I, me

hand

83

手 + 戈 = 我 + 羊 = 義
hand   lance   me   sheep   righteousness

戈

*lance,
spear head*

When Cain and Abel reached adulthood, each was responsible for his own act of worship. So it was on one occasion that Cain decided to offer some of his assorted beautiful fruits in the place of a lamb. "In the course of time Cain brought to the Lord an offering of the fruit of the ground, and Abel brought of the firstlings of his flock and of their fat portions" (Genesis 4:3, 4). At the same time the younger brother Abel came leading a lamb, which he then killed and placed upon his altar. Both young men knelt before their altars, awaiting the signal that their offerings were acceptable. "And the Lord had regard for Abel and his offering" (Genesis 4:4). It would appear that God sent a fire from heaven that burned up the lamb, for from the narrative it is apparent that there was some visible sign of acceptance of the gift.[2] When Abel's lamb was consumed, he arose and left to return to his flock.

Cain remained on his knees, still awaiting this special sign. But there was no visible indication that Cain's offering of fruit was accepted. At last he arose, angry with God. As he left in bitterness, Genesis records that God called to him and said, " 'Why are you angry, and why has your countenance fallen? If you do well, will you not be accepted? And if you do not do well, sin is couching at the door; its desire is for you, but you must master it' " (Genesis 4:6, 7). If Cain had thought to do things his own way, he soon discovered that his own fruit offering was not accepted.

Instead of repenting of his presumptuous and diso-bedient act, Cain became more stubborn and defiant.

84

He sought out his brother and took vengeance on him. "Cain said to Abel his brother, 'Let us go out to the field.' And when they were in the field, Cain rose up against his brother Abel and killed him" (Genesis 4:8). Cain had become the world's first murderer!

Usually the brothers returned home together at dusk when their day's work was finished. This evening only Cain returned; and when Abel failed to come, the parents began to question Cain regarding his brother's whereabouts. Not only his parents but also "the Lord said to Cain, 'Where is Abel your brother?' He [Cain] said, 'I do not know; am I my brother's keeper?' And the Lord said, 'What have you done? The voice of your brother's blood is crying to Me from the ground'" (Genesis 4:9, 10).

Obviously Cain was unrepentant and surely deserved the just punishment which God decreed. But listen to their conversation: " 'When you till the ground, it shall no longer yield to you its strength; you shall be a fugitive and a wanderer on the earth.' Cain said to the Lord, 'My punishment is greater than I can bear. . . . Whoever finds me will slay me.' Then the Lord said to him, 'Not so! . . .' And the Lord put a *mark* on Cain, lest any who came upon him should kill him" (Genesis 4:12-15). The Lord showed Cain unmerited mercy — even though Cain, the older brother, was destined to be a vagrant, God promised him protection.

In the Chinese culture the elder brother is shown regard by using the respectful address *elder brother* 兄, rather than calling him by name. He was literally the *spokes* 口 *man* 儿 and important representative for the family, as shown by this character 兄. A similar

elder brother

*cruel, fierce,
inhuman,
violent*

posterity

small, tender

彡

*to follow,
one after
another*

character 兇 has the same pronounciation in the Chinese but means *cruel, fierce, violent, or inhuman* and is used in reference to killing. The figure itself shows a mark on the body, even as Cain, the original *elder brother* and the first *cruel and passionate* murderer had been marked by God. In the Chinese writing 乂 is used in many words to donote killing or cutting. Therefore this mark on the *elder brother* 兇 was very significant in designating him as a murderer. In past years, criminals in China were tattooed on the cheeks or forehead so that for the rest of their lives they would be recognized as outcasts from society. This custom could well have been derived from a knowledge of the ancient story of Cain. It is also surmised that by the broken *mouth* 凵 he was no longer regarded as the spokesman for the family.

"And Adam knew his wife again, and she bore a son and called his name Seth, for she said, 'God has appointed for me another child instead of Abel, for Cain slew him ' " (Genesis 4:25). God's original command to Adam and Eve was that they be fruitful and multiply and replenish the earth (Genesis 1:28). After this, during their long lifetimes of nearly 1,000 years, in the perfection of newly created mankind, the time of childbearing for the women doubtless continued for hundreds of years, instead of the approximate 30 year fertile period of women today. The world was consequently rapidly populated and a fantastic population explosion resulted. The word *posterity, descendants, afterwards* 後 depicts the first *couple* 彳 with something *small, tender* 幺 (a baby), *following, one after another* 夂. They begat posterity afterwards, one after another.

$$彳 \quad + \quad 幺 \quad + \quad 夂 \quad = \quad 後^3$$

two   small   one after   posterity
persons   (baby)   another

Cain afterward built the world's first city. "Cain knew his wife [his sister], and she conceived and bore Enoch, and he built a city, and called the name of the city after the name of his son, Enoch" (Genesis 4:17). In the fifth generation of Cain's descendants, the Bible records a man who was not only a polygamist but also a murderer. Thus the earth, very early, became divided into two factions. The wicked descendants of Cain arrogantly despised and rejected God. But the line of Seth were God-fearing. Of them it is written, "To Seth also a son was born, and he called his name Enosh. At that time men began *to call upon the name of* the Lord" (Genesis 4:26).

This term, "to call upon the name of the Lord," is very significant and has been used in a special way throughout the Bible to indicate those seeking godliness. In the Old Testament it was closely connected with the sacrificial services initiated at the time when God first provided garments of skins and expelled Adam and Eve from their garden home. Often the supplicant was rewarded by the manifestation of fire from heaven consuming the offering.[4]

The *sheep* 羊 was the first sacrificial animal to be specified, and as previously mentioned, represented the Lamb of God, Jesus Christ, the promised Seed of the woman, who was to come in the line of the faithful descendants of Seth. The Chinese and the Hebrews, who were to come years later as the descendants of Abraham, presented these specific animal offerings to one Supreme God.[5] For the Hebrews this God was *Elohim, Yahweh,* or *Shaddai*. His appellation by the Chinese was *Shang Ti* 上帝, meaning very literally, the *emperor* 帝 *above* 上.

sheep

ShangTi, Heavenly Ruler

87

good,
virtuous,
perfect

words

to judge,
to examine
with care

happiness,
auspicious

sacrificial
animals

bullock, ox

beautiful

Note the interesting phonetic similarities between *ShangTi* (also pronounced ShangDai in some dialects) and *Shaddai*!

Close consideration to the calligraphic record of the Chinese will reveal an authentic record of their pristine religious concepts. To suggest anything good or prosperous, the *lamb* 羊 was often used in a character. For example, *good, virtuous, perfect* 善 in the more ancient writing is clearly 譱, where 音 is 言 *words*, and thus the character expresses that the *lamb's words* are *good*. A second way of arranging these radicals 詳 conveys the idea of *examining with care, to judge*, for this is the ultimate prerogative of the Lamb. "He who sat upon it is called Faithful and True, and in righteousness He *judges* and makes war. . . . And the name by which He is called is the *Word* of God" (Revelation 19:11, 13). In another beautiful symbol, *prosperity, happiness, auspicious* 祥, *God* 礻 and the *lamb* 羊 are wedded to create the character representation.

To portray the sinlessness of Christ, only unblemished, perfect, sacrificial animals were used in the Hebrew services. "Take a *bull calf* for a sin offering, and a *ram* for a burnt offering, both *without blemish*, and offer them before the Lord" (Leviticus 9: 2). This verse is exactly duplicated by the Chinese character for *sacrificial animals* 犧 where the animals specified are a *lamb* 羊 and a *bullock, ox* 牛. These beasts must also be unblemished, or *beautiful* 秀.

牛　　＋　　羊　　＋　　秀　　＋　　戈　　＝　　犧
ox　　　　sheep　　beautiful　　spear head　　sacrificial
　　　　　　　　　(unblemished)　　　　　　　　animals

The Chinese and Hebrews surely must have had identical roots in the ancient past, as evidenced by the

88

similarity of their religious rituals. They both observed morning and evening sacrifices. "One lamb you shall offer in the *morning*, and the other lamb you shall offer in the *evening*" (Exodus 29:39). This had great significance, for at the third hour (9 a.m.) Christ was to be hung on the cross (Mark 15:25), the time of the morning sacrifice; and at the ninth hour (3 p.m.) He gave His life (Mark 15:34), when the evening sacrifice was being offered.

evening

"Hsi," *sacrificial animals* 犧 in Chinese, has the same phonetic sound as the word "hsi" *evening* 夕 and "hsi" *west* 西. It would certainly seem that "hsi" indicating the *sacrificial animals* arose phonetically by association with the time of the ritual in the evening. On the other hand, another word for *sacrifice* is 祀, "szu." By itself, the constituent radical 巳 is "szu" and designates time: *9-11 a.m.* "Szu" must therefore be a morning sacrifice. Furthermore, in the more explicit older calligraphy, 祀[6] is written as 𥛸 which portrays *two persons* 𠂇 with uplifted hands worshiping *God* 川 at the *Garden* ⊕ . Evidently outside the gates of Eden was the site where the original altar was set up by Adam.

west

sacrifice

In the Chinese culture the *eldest son or firstborn* 兄 must have been the one who inherited the priestly duties of directing the family to God. It was his privilege *to pray to or invoke* 祝 God on behalf of the others. He was the family *spokes* 口 *man* 儿. In the Hebrew economy, the eldest son also inherited the birthright with its sacred duties.

9-11 a.m.

兄
eldest son

口	+	儿	=	兄	+	礻	=	祝
spokes		*man*		*eldest son*		*God*		*pray, invoke*

祝
to pray, invoke

This tremendous privilege Cain, as the eldest son, had

viewed lightly; he thus despised righteous Abel and his offering, which had been acceptable to God.

You might be thinking, "What is so important about the ancient sacrificial system of the Chinese and why compare this with the Hebrew rituals? After all, many other early cultures had animal sacrifices–even human sacrifices!" In truth, there were a vast number of sacrificial systems with a great variety of animal offerings. But these were a corruption of the original meaningful services designated by God as object lessons. Also, the polytheistic peoples, following in the footsteps of the renegade Cain, offered to a multitude of deities. Only the Hebrews and Chinese were strict monotheists.[7] Only they understood and appreciated the pathos of the ceremonies.

During the long Hebrew sojourn in Egypt, much of this time in bondage when they were allowed no freedom of worship, they largely forgot the religion of their ancestors, Jacob and Abraham, Noah and Adam. They had lost sight of the significance of the sacrifices and even the ultimate promise of a Messiah. These rites were reinstituted for the Hebrews at Mount Sinai following the great exodus from Egypt, about 1445 B.C. Meanwhile, by this time in China, the original ceremonies were still being faithfully practiced but with little comprehension of the true intent of the offerings, and with considerable adulteration by a growing ancestral worship.

The Chinese actually continued these sacrificial rituals into modern times! The Manchu dynasty extended from A.D. 1644 to A.D. 1911; and with the creation of the Republic of China in 1912, China's monarchal rule ended for all time. The emperors of this last dynasty still annually engaged in the interesting "border" ceremony of antiquity. At the time of the winter solstice, two hours before midday (refer to the character, *sacrifice* 祀 which denotes the time, 9-11 a.m.), the Chinese monarch left the royal palace in a ritual chariot that carried him to the *T'ien Tan*. This great, square, elevated "Temple to Heaven" in Peking is thus described:

> Within the gates of the southern division of the capital, and surrounded by a sacred grove so extensive that the silence of its deep shades is never broken by the noises of the busy world, stands the Temple of Heaven. It consists of a single tower, whose tiling of resplendent azure is intended to represent the form and color of the aerial vault. It contains no image, and the solemn rites are not performed within the tower; but, on a marble altar which stands before it, a bullock is offered once a year as a burnt-sacrifice, while the master of the Empire prostrates himself in adoration of the Spirit of the Universe.[8]

The public offering of this sacrifice was the chief evidence of the right to rule. Consequently, the practice was strictly observed by the ruling sovereign down through the ages.

The significance of the sacrifice had long since been completely lost. It was merely thought to be an "old custom." Even Confucius nearly 2,500 years before had been ignorant of its origin, although he researched with keenest interest into the meaning of this sacrifice.

He attached so much importance to it as to declare that "the man who could explain the sacrifice to God would be able to rule the Empire as easily as he could look on the palm of his own hand."[9]

Although the origin and meaning of this ancient ceremony have been lost sight of by the Chinese, the mere fact of its existence and practice for nearly 4,500 years, together with the miracle of its survival into the 20th century from ancient times as a sacrifice to the Supreme God, *ShangTi*, is indeed incredible!

The marvelous fact is that from the Chinese culture, geographically and ethnically widely separated from the Hebrew nation, similar details of worship were preserved. These may be added as an additional link in the lengthening chain which binds the two peoples and further substantiates and verifies the early chapters of Genesis as revealed truth!

Chapter 9: A Bleak World

That there ever was a universal flood has been all but discounted by modern man. How is it then that nearly every ancient civilization on earth has a flood epic recording a catastrophic deluge? These flood stories, however, have been interpreted as either localized events involving only a small segment of the earth, or as mythological tales. Yet, if all of these widely scattered cultures cite a deluge, the likelihood that the entire world suffered together from the same event is compounded. As the descendants of the survivors again dispersed over the face of the earth, they must have carried the memory of this universal cataclysm with them as a part of their historical past.

Aside from these ancient records, apparent physical evidences, worldwide in scope, can be found, mute witnesses of this destructive upheaval. Petrified forests, coal and oil deposits, fossil remains of now extinct mammoth animals, deep eroded canyons, subterranean caverns, massive folds in the earth's strata, widespread volcanic residue, and many other phenomena in all parts of the earth indicate a former terrestrial catastrophe, which completely changed the face of this world of ours. Whereas the modern world is probably less than one-tenth habitable because of mighty globe-encircling seas and untenable weather conditions, icy wastes and vast arid deserts, steaming insect-infested jungles and massive sky-high mountain chains, this was not always so, as the various remnants of the former world testify.

Attempts to explain scientifically a flood of such total proportions have been made. One popular theory is a near astral collision with gravitational conflict resulting in heaving oceans, surging tides, and lava movement in the earth's crust causing violent eruptions with mountain-building.[1] By whatever causal agents and physical means it might have been effected, the Biblical reason for the flood is given very simply in the Genesis record. "The Lord saw that the wickedness of man was great in the earth, and that every imagination of the thoughts of his heart was only evil continually. . . . And God said to Noah, 'I have determined to make an end of all flesh; for the earth is filled with violence through them; behold I will destroy them with the earth. Make yourself an ark of gopher wood. . . . For behold, I will bring a flood of waters upon the earth, to destroy all flesh in which is the breath of life from under heaven; everything that is on the earth shall die. But I will establish my covenant with you; and you shall come into the ark, you, your sons [Ham, Shem and Japheth], your wife, and your sons' wives with you'" (Genesis 6:5, 13, 14, 17, 18).

We might get a picture of an angry God with patience worn thin, because His creatures failed to obey His every dictate. This is the portrait that Lucifer would paint. However, instead, it was a disappointed God, aghast at the wickedness and violence conjured by the human race, which He had wanted so much to be perfect and holy! For yet another 120 years (Genesis 6:3), God tolerated sinful mankind while Noah and his sons under God's direction built the mighty ark. Noah was the 10th generation from Adam, and according to the chronology of the genealogies (Genesis 5:3-30), it was about the year 1656 after creation when God allowed the devastating flood to sweep over the earth.

The ark, a tremendous vessel — 450 feet long, 75 feet broad, and 45 feet high, (Genesis 6:15 Moffat), such as no man had ever seen before, was to become a refuge during the terrible storm. The Chinese character for *boat* 船[2] gives this very representation. There are three elements pictured: a *vessel* 舟, *eight* 八, and mouth 口, meaning "people." The word for boat, then, tells the story of this first great ark which, in spite of the years of warning and pleading by Noah to his compatriots, had just eight passengers. "And Noah and his sons [Ham, Shem, and Japheth] and his wife and his sons' wives with him, went into the ark, to escape the waters of the flood" (Genesis 7 : 7).

船
boat

舟
vessel

八
eight

One finds that these original eight people from whom the earth was repopulated after the flood, play a very important and prominent role in many Chinese characters. It has been pointed out several times that this earth has known two very different worlds, the first a perfect creation extending from the time of Adam and Eve until it was completely destroyed and buried by the devastating flood. Many of the characters which were derived from episodes involving Adam and Eve during the antediluvian times had incorporated in them various symbols represen-

95

ting this first couple, such as 二, 口 口, 呂, 火火 , 炎, 亻 or 大 . Now as the postdiluvian events are studied, it will be seen that, instead of featuring the original progenitor pair, the eight survivors of the flood are memorialized in the same way. They now become the new ancestors of all future generations, and hence the numeral *eight* becomes as important in reference to the postdiluvian stories as the figure *two* was to antediluvian epics. *Eight*, it will be seen, also takes a variety of forms: 八 , 儿 , or 八 , whichever best accommodates the space, shape, or whim of artistic smartness desired in a character.

八
儿
八
eight

The ark had been completed and supplied with provisions. Now the dramatic moment arrived when "The Lord said to Noah, 'Go into the ark, you and all your household, for I have seen that you are righteous before Me in this generation. Take with you seven pairs of all clean animals, the male and his mate; and a pair of the animals that are not clean, the male and his mate; and seven pairs of the birds of the air also, male and female, to keep their kind alive upon the face of all the earth. For in seven days I will send rain upon the earth forty days and forty nights; and every living thing that I have made I will blot out from the face of the ground.' And Noah did all that the Lord had commanded him" (Genesis 7:1-5).

rain

Rain 雨 had never been experienced before by the antediluvians, "For the Lord God had not caused it to rain upon the earth, . . . But a mist went up from the earth and watered the whole face of the ground" (Genesis 2:5, 6). Those unrepentant and wicked men who had refused the oft-given invitation to enter the ark were now terrified to see great drops of water falling from the sky, and as the storm raged, "all the fountains of the great deep burst forth, and the windows of the heavens were opened" (Genesis 7:11). Note again the radicals for *water* 水 and 氵. Do these not resemble fountains of water rising to a height and falling back in all directions? It is interesting that the ancient forms also portray *water* 巛 , 巛 most often vertical, instead of horizontal, as expected.

water

Man and beast alike struggled to escape the rising waters, but at last all were engulfed as the waters *covered over* 弇 all. This figure further describes men's confederacy against God, as 合 indicates *all, or united*, and 廾 is a radical for *hands joined together*, suggesting not only their united rebellion but also the attempt to help each other escape the threatening waters. When *water* 氵 is added to 弇, the combined symbol forms the word, *to drown, to overflow, submerged* 渰 .

cover over

all, united

廾

hands joined, together

合 + 廾 = 弇 + 氵 = 渰 [3]
united　hands　cover　water　drown
　　　joined　over

to drown

A word, *total, or altogether* 共, is significant in that it indicates that the *eight* 八 people were the total population of the earth to be delivered from the overflowing waters. The remaining portions of the figure represent *hands joined* 廾 , and the horizontal line, the *earth* 一 . This would picture a company of *eight* united people, with *hands joined* 廾 , forming the *total* 共 [4] number. If the radical *water* 氵 is added to this same figure, the new character formed is *flood* 洪, also meaning *vast*. This ideograph therefore reveals a great

共

total, altogether

洪

flood, vast

truth, that the flood involving these *eight* people was *total*, or universal, and not a localized catastrophe.

八 + 廾 + 一 = 共 + 氵 = 洪
eight + *united* + *earth* = *total* + *water* = *flood*

An early pictograph of *flood* is exactly comparable:

Note also
the water
"covering"
the earth.

hands joined
water
earth
eight

洪

Another explicitly shows the four hands of the males united and "riding" above the waters: 嬜 . "And the waters prevailed so mightily upon the earth that *all the high mountains under the whole heaven were covered*" (Genesis 7:19). This verse could be interpreted only as a universal, total *deluge*.

to hand down, to continue

Still another character depicting the *eight* 几 *people* 口 is 沿 meaning variously *to hand down*, *to continue*, *to follow a course*. Note several interesting methods of writing the old forms: 㳂 , 㳂 , or 㳂 . In this last figure, the *eight persons* 㳂 are seen floating *on* the *water* ≋ . It was, of course, from these eight persons that all tradition, history, and knowledge have *continued* from the first world into the second, being "handed down."

"The waters prevailed and increased greatly upon the earth; and the ark floated on the face of the waters. ... And the waters prevailed upon the earth a hundred and fifty days" (Genesis 7:18, 24). At the end of this 150-day period the ark came to rest on the mountains of Ararat (Genesis 8:4), but it would be many months before the earth had dried sufficiently to permit their leaving the ark. One year and 10 days after the rain had begun to descend, God commanded Noah to leave the ark. "The waters were dried from off the earth; and Noah removed the covering of the ark, and looked, and behold, the face of the ground was dry" (Genesis 8:13). But what a bleak and different world met their eyes! The beautiful trees and all vegetation were gone. Before them were rugged, snow-covered mountains; bare hills; and exposed craggy rocks lining dangerous canyons, flowing with rushing, receding, muddy rivers. A cold wind whistled around the ark. The pleasant, verdant, temperate land they had known before had been buried, and in its place was a desolate, strange earth, unrecognizable and ugly.

The first act that Noah performed after he and his family left the ark was to offer sacrifices of thanksgiving to God that their lives were preserved. "Then Noah built an altar to the Lord, and took of every clean animal and of every clean bird, and offered burnt offerings on the altar" (Genesis 8:20). Once again the symbolic *sacrifices* 祭 were continued, as animals *(flesh)* 月 were offered *again* 又 to *God* 示.

to sacrifice

月	+	又	+	示	=	祭 [5]
flesh (animal)		again		God		to sacrifice

flesh

again

The desolate new world which met the remnant's gaze required coinage of words to describe the changed conditions. A new way of life also emerged, necessitating additional vocabulary with corresponding words that could be used as ideograms. Accordingly, the Chinese appear to have incorporated the *eight* progenitors of this second world into many characters descriptive of the altered conditions.

cave

When Noah's family left the ark, they may have lived in a large cave hollowed out by the receding waters, for there were no trees with which to build a house. At least the Chinese seem to have pictured them as living in a *cave* 穴, as this figure would indicate, for it is composed undeniably of a *roof* 宀 with the figure *eight* 八 under it.

宀 + 八 = 穴

roof,   *eight*   *cave*
house

work

Since all of the earth's vegetation had been washed away, it was necessary for the family to begin to plant seed and gardens in order to grow food to sustain themselves. When the eight kinsmen went to work in the fields, the cave, of course, was empty. Thus, by adding *work* 工 to the *cave* 穴, the character *empty, hollow* 空 is formed—nobody is at home in the cave. They have all gone to work.

空

empty, hollow

eight   *roof*   *cave*   *work*   *empty*

So that no one need guess that the vertical line | in *work* 工 represented a *person*, *hair* 彡 is added in an earlier character 𢒉.

common to all, public

The *eight* 八 common ancestors of today's world population are seen in the character 公 meaning *common to all*, *public*, which would surely define nicely the members of Noah's family. The word 公 also carries the more colloquial meaning of *grandfather* (the husband's father). This could well have applied to Noah himself as the grandfather of all living. A *certain person* 厶 is derived as a shortened form of *mouth, person* 口.

厶

a certain person

100

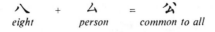

八 + 厶 = 公
eight   person   common to all

Examine another word, *division* 分. One may identify *eight* 八 and a *knife* 刀. The Chinese may have pictured the eight people as having a problem in dividing their possessions after having lived together in the ark for a year. Symbolically, the *knife* is used to do the *dividing* 分.

分

division

It will be noted in the old writing that *eight* 八, itself, characteristically divides into mirror images) (,] [, or 冂, for example; and therefore significantly has become a symbol of *division or separation*. This is well demonstrated in the older forms of 公 as 冏 ; or 分 as 以.

The new way of life touched many areas. The descendants of Noah must *exchange or barter* 兌. Note the *eight* 八 spread far apart to accommodate an *older brother* 兄, who possibly became the spokesman for the family. This figure is incorporated into a larger character meaning *to speak, to tell* 說. This word may have grown out of lengthy *exchange* 兌 of *words* 言 made necessary in business affairs.

兌

to exchange,
barter

説

to speak,
tell, say

八 + 兄 = 兌 + 言 = 說
eight   older   exchange   words   to speak,
        brother   say, tell

This word for *to speak, to say* 說, is probably the most commonly used character today for "talking" and has replaced in the language the radical *to speak* 曰, which has become largely archaic.

Noah suffered disappointment and anguish, even as Adam had, in seeing one of his sons become disrespectful and wicked. His youngest son, Ham, was separated from the family, even as Cain had been. The curse that fell upon Ham and his posterity was to become the servants of his brothers. It was through this new rebellious line also that the first postflood cities would be built.

Shem, on the other hand, was chosen because of his fidelity, as the son through whom the promised Seed would eventually come. His later descendants, Abraham Jacob, Judah, David, and Solomon preserved a knowledge of God in the earth as the Hebrew people.

It might be assumed that the ancient Chinese were rather immediate descendants of Noah, as evidenced by their familiarity with the story of the flood. Consequently it would be natural for the inventor of the Chinese characters to incorporate essential facts regarding the deluge and the human remnant of eight people into a newly developing calligraphy. In this way an authentic historical record could be preserved. Even in our day, millennia later, this primitive writing still memorializes the beginnings of the second world and the postdiluvian era by the frequent use of the numeral *eight* in their characters.

Chapter 10 :   The Tower of United Defiance

After the flood, the earth began to be repopulated with the descendants of Noah and his three sons, Shem, Ham, and Japheth. At this time, according to the Genesis record, "The whole earth had *one language* and few words" (Genesis 11:1). Some left the region of Mount Ararat where the ark had grounded as the flood waters subsided and traveled to a fertile valley of Shinar, between the Tigris and Euphrates Rivers, which would later become Mesopotamia. There, several cities were founded, Erech, Accad, Babel, and Calah, by Nimrod, the grandson of Ham (Genesis 10:10).

If Ham's grandson, Nimrod, was able to found four cities from the world's total inhabitants after such a short time, there must have been a great burst of population immediately after the flood. The generation time had been shortened from about 100 years in the antediluvian patriarchs to only 30 years immediately after the flood. At the time the Chinese race came into being after the flood, the 30-year generation time was already a fact and is thus recorded as *an age, a generation of 30*

103

世

*an age, a
generation
of 30 years*

years, from generation to generation 世. Usually 30 is written 三十 (three tens), occasionally as 卅 . Written as it is with a base line 世, the word indicates a unit of 30 years.

The period of fertility must have been very long for the early vigorous descendants whose total lifetimes were about 400 years. The original eight survivors of the flood themselves bore many children also, as it is recorded that Noah lived 350 years and Shem 500 years after the flood.

In one of Nimrod's cities, Babel, something occurred that was to forever change the course of civilization. As the abbreviated genealogic record of Shem is read in Genesis 10, one meets the name of Peleg in the fifth generation from Noah. Of him it is said, "The name of one was Peleg; for in his days *the earth was divided*" (Genesis 10:25). Anciently, the names of children had great significance. Sometimes these revealed the character traits of a child; other names were prophetic, as "Methuselah," for example, which meant "at his death the sending forth of waters." He died in the year of the flood, 1656 years after creation. Peleg's name meant "division." Of Shem's lineage, he evidently was born the year of the great dispersion, which was a mere 101 years following the flood, according to the carefully recorded genealogy of Genesis 11. How many adult people might there have been by this time with the above reproductive facts in mind? A conservative estimate is at least several thousand people.

By now men were quite clever with their building talents, for they had learned not only how to make clay

104

bricks but to increase the durability of this building material by firing it. They had also developed a suitable mortar for cementing the bricks together to construct impressive edifices. While laying out the city of Babel, they also began to erect a tower that was to become very noteworthy. Towers were at this point in history, quite fashionable as temples of worship but, unfortunately, not a place to worship the God of heaven and Creator of the earth. Already men had departed from the services established by God,and instead had substituted the deification of wooden, stone, and metal idols, as well as the sun, moon, and stars. These inanimate images were placed in the temple towers for adoration.[1]

The purpose in constructing this particular ziggurat in Babel, however, was probably dual — not only to house their false gods, but also as an object of rebellion against the true God. The dwellers in Babel determined that never again would a destructive flood come upon mankind for they bragged, "Come, let us build ourselves a city, and a tower with its top in the heavens, and *let us make a name for ourselves*, lest we be scattered abroad upon the face of the whole earth" (Genesis 11:4). Instead of "call [ing] upon the name of the Lord" (Genesis 4:26) in true worship, they determined to "make a name for themselves," and independently substitute their own gods or works —even as their defiant ancestors Cain and Ham had done. Was this also to be an escape tower should another flood come? Evidently the people had forgotten God's promise to Noah, "I will remember My covenant which is between Me and you and every living creature of all flesh; and the waters shall never again become a flood to destroy all flesh" (Genesis 9:15). Either they had forgotten this promise, or they did not believe it!

How significant that the Chinese word for *tower* 塔 is a shorthand record of this project. On the left side of the figure, artistically accommodating itself to the slope of the tower is the radical 土 *dirt, clay,* of which the bricks were made. They had boasted, " 'Come, let us make bricks, and burn them thoroughly.' And they had brick for stone, and bitumen for mortar" (Genesis 11:3). Then they *united, joined together* 合 in their rebellion against God. The Chinese placed upon the pinnacle of the *tower* 塔 the sign of Adam's curse ⧾ , recognizing the folly of this venture. (It would be unlikely that *weeds* ⧾ would grow on top of a brick tower!) One other aspect of the character might also have importance. They were originally all of one speech: *men* 人 ; *one* 一 ; *speech* 口 . Adding the *grass* on the top, 荅 means *to undertake.* The Chinese themselves built no towers or pagodas until the Buddhist era.[2] This character for *tower* 塔 must surely, therefore, refer to the Tower of Babel.

人 + 一 + 口 = 合 + ⧾ = 荅 + 土 = 塔

mankind   *one*   *mouth*   *united*   *grass*   *undertake*   *clay*   *tower*
               (speech)   *(brick)*

So the work on the tower began, but God was displeased at their rebellious attitude and decided to put an end to their scheme with a very clever plan of His own. "And the Lord came down to see the city and the tower, which the sons of men had built. And the Lord said, 'Behold, they are one people, and they have all one language; and this is only the beginning of what they will do; and nothing that they propose to do will now

106

be impossible for them. Come, let us go down, and there *confuse their language*, that they may not understand one another's speech'"(Genesis 11:5-7). He proceeded to do just that, and as a result of the confounded language there was nothing else to do but to stop work on the uncompleted tower, for no one could understand the other's orders or requests, and all was in great turmoil.

Again the Chinese have a word which amazingly means not only *confusion* but also *rebellion* 乱. This succinctly tells the story in just two pictures. The *tongue* 舌 was confused when God changed the language of the rebels. "And the Lord said, 'Behold they are one people, and they have all one language. . . . Come, let us go down, and there confuse their language, that they may not understand one another's speech' "(Genesis 11:6,7). The right hand part of the character portrays the *right leg* ㇄ [3] extended for walking. It will be seen that this is half of the radical for *man* 儿. Since their *tongues* 舌 [4] were speaking new languages, there was nothing left to do in this frustrating situation, but to *strike out and journey* to a new place of their own.

rebellion,
confusion

舌
tongue

㇄
[*right leg*,]
(*half of* 儿)

$$舌 + ㇄ = 乱$$

| *tongue* | [*right leg*] | *rebellion, confusion* |

As Moses put it: "Therefore its name was called Babel, because there the Lord confused the language of all the earth; and from there the Lord scattered them abroad over the face of all the earth" (Genesis 11:9).

The natural result of the confusion of the language was exactly what they had hoped would never happen! They left the city in small bands of people who could understand each other, probably by families, as delineated in Genesis 10 and 11. In this way, Babel got its name meaning "confusion," since it was here that the Lord mixed up the language. It was thus that the great dispersion of people began and the various ethnic divisions of mankind developed. Surely it was a tremendously historical milestone to warrant giving a newborn son the name "Peleg" — "Division." Recall the character meaning *division* 分, which contained the *eight* 八 ancestors and a *knife* 刀, a symbolic instrument for "dividing." Here it is clear that from the *eight* stem the diversified future world population, at the time of the *Division* 分.

division,
to separate

The "dispersion" was truly a great pivotal point in antiquity for the event to be recorded in the Genesis annals, and for the Chinese to fashion several ideograms corresponding to the momentous incident.

The numeral *four* 四 also stems from *eight* 几 being divided in four directions 口. This is supported also by the earlier calligraphy, as 冗, 囗 or the interesting figure 𝄀𝄀 which shows a double dividing of the numeral *eight*.

four

The radical *four* 四 is often used together with a second character meaning to *scatter, to disperse* 散. Note the top left portion 辻, which appears to be an abbreviation of 共, meaning *total or all*. The 月, *flesh*, must signify "people or mankind," possibly related to families. The last radical is *to follow* 攵. This character, *to disperse* 散, could indicate then that *all flesh* (families) *followed*. Used with the numeral *four* 四, 四散 signifies *scattered in four directions*.

to scatter,
disperse

all (abbrev.)

flesh
(people)

to follow

辻	+	月	+	攵	=	散[5]
all (abbrev.)		flesh (families)		followed		scatter, disperse

It is likely, since their historical date of origin coincides closely with this point in time, that the ancestors of the Chinese people left the valley of Shinar in the great migration and journeyed eastward, to soon settle in the fertile land of China. A retrospective depiction of their *migration, to remove, to shift* 遷, would mean nothing except in the light of the Genesis narrative of chapter 11. It concisely summarizes the event in four radicals. In the *west* 西[6] (Babel) there had been a *great* 大 (大 is spread apart to accommodate the lower figure) *division, separation* 己. This radical, 己, *joint or seal*, is actually half of a larger seal of authority 卩. Breaking the seal in half would indicate a *division or separation* 己. This *division* resulted in their *walking* 辶 in a great migratory move.

west

大 + 己 + 西 + 辶 = 遷
great [division] west walking migration

great

A second form for *migration* is 迁, which very simply reveals that *thousands* 千 are *walking* 辶. Notice that the *thousand* 千 has a "p'ieh" 丿 , indicating movement, and this event possibly marks the origin of this numeral. It is interesting also to note that *tongue* 舌 has a *thousand* 千 issuing from the *mouth* 口. This word could likewise very well have original reference to the Babel story dealing specifically with the tongue. The character 迁 is not as specific as the former character indicating the origin of the *migration* in the *west* 西, but it does tell the large number of those removing in various directions, possibly the greatest mass dispersion the earth has ever seen.

Thus it likely happened that the progenitors of the Chinese people immigrated to the Far East, carrying

to migrate

thousand

将 division (of seal)

辶 walking

109

with them direct word-of-mouth knowledge of the early beginnings on earth, and of the Creator, the true God, whom they came to call *ShangTi.*

Perhaps the wise old sage who was given the assignment by his king of inventing a written language for the new nation had even been present as a young man at the Tower of Babel and had witnessed the profound effect upon the confederate rebels when their common mother tongue was suddenly confused and communications were broken down. There had been days or turmoil when families speaking the same tongue were organizing themselves into bands. Finally, the companies of people dispersed in all directions. His compatriots had made the lengthy, hard migration as far as possible to the east, where they hoped for isolation and a new beginning. He had received the total historical background by word-of-mouth, possibly even from Noah or Shem themselves; then with his own more recent personal experiences to use as familiar facts, he cleverly added to the written language. Only a pictographic and ideographic language could so perfectly preserve history in such accurate detail.

One might even question whether the Chinese themselves took part in the rebellion at Babel. Since they were the only worshipers of the Supreme Ruler of Heaven, other than the Shemites, and since they had such a high moral code, along with rituals similar to the Shemites, might they have had the same fraternal roots? It is entirely conjectural, but they may have taken this opportunity to leave the polytheistic environment of Babel and join in the dispersion simply from the standpoint of wanting to separate themselves from nonbelievers.

Study suggests that the Chinese forebears summarized the three great rebellions of early mankind by indicating that the recalcitrants *united as one* 合 in their defiance of God. Note this figure in the following characters. For Adam and Eve, the first rebels, there was the *flaming sword* 劍 which prevented them from repossessing Eden. The antediluvians, who entered into mass malcontent and disbelief, were *drowned* 滔 by the flood, while the bold seditionists at the *Tower* 塔 of Babel had their tongues confounded. In each of these instances, with corresponding commemorating characters, the *confederacy* 合 and determination to act independently and to separate themselves from God, can be seen.

to unite
as one

Even the punishment decreed by God for these great rebellions of mankind was measured out with a mixture of blessing. The "thorns and thistles" allotted to Adam and Eve kept them and all mankind busy with honest labor. The punishment of the antediluvian world changed the face of the entire earth and all weather conditions. But even the flood, with the burial of tremendous amounts of organic matter from both plant and animal sources, has proven a boon to modern man who benefits from the resultant oil and coal deposits.

sword

drown

The dispersion at the tower of Babel again may have been seen as a curse by the wicked who had their rebellious plans thwarted, and the differences in language throughout the world have been a continuing impediment to understanding and communication. On the other hand, the Babel migration was a means of repopulating the entire earth, and was actually an advantage to some, such as the Chinese who could isolate themselves in a distant land and carry on worship to the true

塔

tower

God without molestation. This they apparently did for 2,000 years, although the people gradually lost sight of the meaning of their worship, which became a mere ceremony. With the loss of understanding of their rituals, the way was opened for acceptance of new religious innuendos and the introduction of Taoism, Confucianism, and Buddhism.

Epilog . . . Revelation

The mural mosaic at the far end of the Singapore air terminal waiting room transfixed me that Wednesday morning as I was preparing to leave the city after my most recent visit with Pastor Kang. The lighting was perfect so that the portrayed scenic view of the city of Singapore at night, reflected in the foreground harbor waters, was very real. I ascended the stairs to the mezzanine overlooking the rushing, noisy, oblivious throng below and stood there for a long moment, taking it all in — the silhouetted familiar skyline, with scattered lighted windows depicting the ceaseless activity of this Oriental metropolis; the last shades of fading day at the horizon in a cloud-tinted darkening sky; the flickering lights of harbor boats. Why had I not noticed the beauty of this mosaic artistry before on my many trips through Singapore during the more than 10 years since the erection of this new airport?

I walked around the balcony and stood before the immense mural. Now it had become a mass of tiny vari-colored, one-inch tiles mortared into the wall. I gently touched the unevenly set ceramic pieces — "Rather crude!" I thought. It was more difficult at this close range to make out the various objects which composed the panorama. Certainly at this short distance it lacked beauty, the outlines were difficult to delineate, and there was no breath-taking attractiveness. Instead, one might be tempted to criticize the handiwork of the one who had set the tiles in a slightly irregular fashion. Once again I moved away to the far end of the mezzanine, and the city became alive! It was the distance and the lighting. From whence the light came, I do not remember, whether artificial or by skylight, but it was perfect. I could not help but take out my camera, hoping to record its glowing exquisiteness.

"How like this study we have just completed," I mused. "The isolated Chinese character by itself, or perhaps a small series on one aspect of the Genesis subject is interesting, but one might question, 'Is it possible?' or 'Was this really the original intention?' One can become very 'picky' and critical. However, taken as a whole, with all the pieces in place, and with a retrospection of 4,500 years, the total picture becomes amazing!"

I was soon settled comfortably, smoothly airborne. The roar of the jet motors was left far behind with only the whistling wind accompaniment as a reminder of being rapidly transported. The landscape far below was one which I always loved in the Orient — neat patchwork of the rice paddies in their many shades of green, interspersed with unplanted, plowed fields. An aerial view, reflecting the light from the flooded plots, always reminded me of a mammoth stained-glass window.

Perhaps it was this scene that flashed to mind the radical 田 , which we had always used to represent the

Garden of Eden. "Honestly now, doesn't it look more like a well-irrigated and marked out farm? But it must refer to the Garden specifically," I argued to myself, "for such characters as *devil* 鬼, *fruit* 果, *naked* 裸, *happiness* 福, and *tempter* 魔, using 田 , could have no other reference!

garden

"But wait, wasn't the Garden of Eden 'watered?' " Now I remembered a river, in fact, four rivers being mentioned in the oft-read Genesis description. Why had this not seemed important before? I reached for my heavy briefcase and struggled to release it from under the seat in front. I extracted a Bible from my bulging luggage and turned to Genesis 2:9-14. Yes, the river was four-headed and appeared to originate in the center of the Garden near the tree of life and the tree of the knowledge of good and evil. I thought again of the symbol for *garden* 田. "Perfect! A four-headed river originating in the center of the Garden would certainly 'water' it. But what would be its source?

"The head of most rivers is spring *water* — a fountain! Even the radicals for *water* 水, 氵 (older forms 川, 巛 too), are all vertical figures, as though arising from the ground. 水 and 巛 might even be interpreted as flowing in four directions. A fountain! That's it! The Bible is full of verses referring to the 'fountain of life.' " I leafed through the concordance in the back of my Bible and looked under *Fountain*. My eyes fell on something interesting in Song of Solomon 4:12, 15:

water

> A garden locked is my sister, my bride,
> A garden locked, a fountain sealed. . . .
> A garden fountain, a well of living water,
> And flowing streams from Lebanon.

"That's obviously the Garden of Eden after the Fall, 'a garden locked,' and it has a fountain of 'living water' with flowing 'streams!' The 'garden' was also called a 'bride'!" My excitement mounted. "Now, why is the garden square?" for "squareness"[1] did not fit my preconceived mental imagery of Eden.

Turning to Revelation 21 and 22, which I recalled also mentioned the tree of life in the heavenly Paradise, things rapidly began to fit into place. Associated with the tree of life again was the "river of life" that flowed from God's throne—something I had never really understood. Of course God's throne would be in the very center of the Holy City, the New Jerusalem, so beautifully described by the prophet John. Christ's youngest disciple, now grown old and at this writing a prisoner on Patmos, saw in vision a "four square," golden city, surrounded by walls furbished with 12 kinds of shining gems set in the foundations.

Again my mind shifted to another cubical structure —the Most Holy Place of the portable sanctuary, erected from God's explicit specifications given to Moses on Mount Sinai after the exodus from Egypt. God had commanded (Exodus 25 : 8), "Let them make me a sanctuary, that *I may dwell in their midst.*" The beautiful tentlike structure was set up in the very center of the Israelite encampment with the various tribes (families) arranged in definite and orderly positions, forming a greater square. The tabernacle had two apartments. The smaller was four-square, the measurements of length, width, and height, being equal. In it reposed the sacred golden "ark," a chest surmounted by elegantly wrought golden angels, hovering over the "mercy seat." A glorious light shone out from between the angels, representing God's very presence there. This "mercy seat" must be analogous to God's throne (Exodus 25:17-22).

Inside the golden ark were deposited the Ten Commandments, written in stone by the finger of God Himself. There were also two other objects that I had not previously really given thought to. These were "Aaron's rod that budded" and a "golden pot of manna" (Hebrews 9:4). Could Aaron's rod have a symbolic meaning? Here was a dead stick that had miraculously been made to bud with blossoms and bear almonds (Numbers 17:6-8). This may be symbolic of that wonderful tree of life! And the pot of manna, of course, reminds us of Christ Himself, who said, in reply to questions about the manna: "The bread of God is that which comes down from heaven, and gives life to the world. . . . I am the bread of life; he who comes to Me shall not hunger, and he who believes in Me shall never *thirst*" (John 6:33-35). (Compare "thirst" with "living water" in John 4:7-15.)

The square figure with which reference was made to the Garden was beginning to mean something; the celestial Holy City; the Most Holy Place in the wilderness sanctuary with surrounding square Israelite encampment; God's dwelling place and meeting place with man.

The description of the temple seen in vision by Ezekiel was next recalled. Chapter 47 depicts water streaming from under the temple at the side of the altar. The inner room, the Most Holy Place, of the temple was also built in a square. The stream issuing from the temple became a great river, and trees with 12 kinds of fruit and leaves for healing were found along its bank—again, the same imagery. But Revelation 21:22-25 further states that there is "no temple in the [heavenly] city, for its temple is the Lord God the Almighty and the Lamb." It also says that there is no night there, for the glory of God is its light. More pieces are fitted into the jigsaw puzzle.

But now I wanted to focus on the New Testament Messiah, represented by such a multitude of symbols and types in the Old Testament. Why did He say to the woman at the well in Samaria, "Whoever drinks of the water that I shall give him will never thirst; the water that I shall give him will become in him a *spring of water* welling up to *eternal life*" (John 4:14)? How incredible that the Chinese in the character for *eternal* 永 obviously uses the *water* 水 radical! A *point* ﹀ at the top of the figure 永 signifies an "anointing" or "dedication."

water

eternal

On two occasions Jesus fed multitudes of 4 and 5,000 who had gathered to hear Him talk. He broke a few small loaves of bread, providing more than enough for all so that baskets of leftover bread were collected afterward. He exclaimed that only those who "ate His flesh and drank His blood" could be His disciples. This was hard to understand. Even His own disciples failed to grasp its meaning fully until after His death.

tree

Now we move to Calvary. A cross — *a tree* 木 — was erected with Jesus nailed to it. This was the Man known by the multitudes for His miracles and teachings; envied by His brothers for His virtue; loved by His followers for His wise, kind, and gentle manner; hated by the priests for His authority, which was interpreted as blasphemy when He said, "Your sins are forgiven," and for His claim to be the Son of God.

118

The very elements of nature could not endure seeing God's Son so cruelly treated. The day became mysteriously dark and ominous. When He breathed His last, He expressed it in the words: "It is finished!" and He committed Himself into His Father's hands. Not believing He was already dead, a Roman soldier pierced His side, and there came out blood and water. THE SACRIFICE OF THE AGES WAS COMPLETE. The Seed of the Woman had been bruised. The unblemished *Lamb* 羊 of God had given His divine life for all — the Bread was broken, and there was more than enough for everyone. The *Water of Life* had gushed out "for with Thee is the fountain of life" (Psalm 36:9). *The Cross of Calvary had become the Tree of Life to all who would partake!*

羊

lamb

These three figures: the *tree* 木, the *lamb* 羊, and *eternal* 永 (*water* 水) are united into one glorious character meaning *example, pattern* 樣! What more appropriate, complete, and meaningful symbolism could be used to portray our great Exemplar? It would seem that the ancient Chinese sage was truly inspired to draw together these completely symbolic figures and produce a totally meaningful character. He surely appears to have been thinking God's thoughts after Him!

樣

pattern,
example

But the story is hardly finished, for in Revelation 21, we find a tremendous event yet to take place. The Holy City of God, adorned as a bride for her husband (remember the garden as a bride in the Song of Solomon), will descend to the new earth. We read in many scriptures that the earth will again be cleansed from iniquity, not by water but by fire. This is preceded by the mighty, visible, second advent of Jesus to redeem the faithful from this earth. Then they, with Christ, will return in the Holy City (Revelation 21: 1-6) to the new earth, which will be created following the destructive fire. "The heavens and earth that now exist have been stored up for fire, being kept until the day of judgment and destruction of ungodly men. ... The heavens will be kindled and dissolved, and the elements will melt with fire! But according to His promise we wait for new heavens and a new earth in which righteousness dwells" (2 Peter 3: 7, 12, 13). Eden will once more become the meeting place of man with God, this time at His throne in the center of the Holy City.

句

*Imperial
Domain*

勹

to wrap up

God's throne must be the center of the whole universe. How fitting then that in the Chinese character for *imperial domain* 句 is seen the *Garden* of Eden! The radical, *to wrap up* 勹 , looks like a giant hand gathering up the *Garden* of Eden 句, "wrapping it up." to become the future capital of the New Earth, the *Imperial Domain*, God's eternal dwelling place.

> On that day His feet shall stand on the Mount of Olives which lies before Jerusalem on the east; and the Mount of Olives shall be split in two from east to west by a very wide valley. ... then the Lord your God will come, and all the holy ones with Him. On that day there shall be neither cold nor frost. And there shall be continuous day. . . . On that day living waters shall flow out from Jerusalem, half of these to the eastern sea and half of them to the western sea. And the Lord will become king over all the earth (Zechariah 14:4, 5, 6, 8, 9).

Now stand back and look at the entire mosaic of the "City" from a distance. The light has to be adjusted

120

right or one is not attracted to its beauty. All of the time should not be spent absorbed in examining the details, for in so doing, one is apt to become critical and near sighted. Unless the entire picture is seen and in focus, one cannot envision what the Master Artist and Creator has really intended. It has taken the perspective of millennia to catch the true glory of the scene, to put it all together, and grasp the inspiring magnificence and total loveliness of what God has been trying to tell preoccupied and self-centered mankind in a multitude of ways for 6,000 years!

God loved the world so much that He provided the way from a temporal existence to eternal life through His beloved Son, the sacrificial Lamb. The first people in the garden—surrounded by so much righteousness chose death. Subsequent generations have had the way to life prepared, by promise and fulfillment—even while surrounded by so much wrong—through the Tree of the Cross. Whoever accepts the life, death, and resurrection of Christ by faith is invited to partake of the Tree of Life in eternity.

Study Notes and References

Prolog . . . Genesis

1. K. T. Khang (C. H. Kang), *Genesis and the Chinese* (Hong Kong: Independent Printing, 1950).

2. See Chapter 9, note 2.

3. Edward Reese and Frank R. Klassen, *The Chronological Bible* (Nashville : Regal Publishers, Inc., 1977), p. 17.

4. G. D. Wilder and J.H. Ingram, *Analysis of Chinese Characters* (Taipei: Chin Wen Publishing Co., 1964). See also G. Blakney, *A Course in the Analysis of Chinese Characters* (Shanghai: The Commercial Press, Ltd., 1926); G. Bourgois, *Dictionary and Glossary for the Practical Study of the Japanese Ideographs* (Yokohama: Tokyo-Kyo Bun Kwan Co., n.d.); Leo Wieger, *A History of the Religious Beliefs and Philosophical Opinions of China* (Hsien: Hsien Press, China, 1927); Yuen Ren Chao, *Language and Symbolic Systems* (Cambridge: Cambridge University Press. 1960).

5. Lin Tze Ching, *Ting Jung Liu Shui Tong* (Nanking: Quang Ee, China, 1937).

Chapter 1: Not Without Witness

1. Edwin Yamauchi, *The Stones and the Scriptures* (Philadelphia, Pa.: J. B. Lippincott, 1972), p. 36.

2. John Ross, *The Original Religion of China* (London, Oliphant, Anderson and Ferrier, 1909), pp. 19, 20.

3. Terrien De La Couperie, *The Language of China Before the Chinese* (Taipei: Ch'eng-wen Publishing Co., 1966), p. 114.

4. Yamauchi, pp. 36 - 91.

5. George Alexander and John Dart, "Tablets Shed New Light on the Bible," *Los Angeles Times* (June 7, 1976). See also Giovanni Pettinato, "The Royal Archives of Tell Mardikh - Ebla," *Biblical Archaeologist* 39 (1976), pp. 44 - 52.

6. Ivan T. Sanderson, "Riddle of the Quick-Frozen Giants," *Saturday Evening Post* (Jan. 16, 1960), p. 82. See also Harold G. Coffin, *Creation--Accident or Design?* (Washington, D. C.: Review and Herald Publishing Assoc., 1969), p. 203.

7. Donald W. Patten, *The Biblical Flood and the Ice Epoch* (Seattle, Wash.: Pacific Meridian Publishing Co., 1966), pp. 196-208.

8. Rene Noorbergen, *The Ark File* (Mountain View, Calif.: Pacific Press Publ. Assoc., 1974), p. 66, 114 - 129.

Chapter 2: Imperial Intrigue in the Chinese Dark Ages

1. Terrien De La Couperie, *The Language of China Before the Chinese* (Taipei: Ch'eng-wen Publishing Co., 1966), p. 114.

2. Robert K. Douglas, *The Language and Literature of China* (London: Trubner and Co., 1875), pp. 66, 67.

3. Raymond B. Blakney, *A Course in the Analysis of Chinese Characters* (Shanghai: The Commercial Press, Ltd., 1926), p. 12. See also Douglas, p. 15; R. H. Mathews, *Chinese-English Dictionary* (Cambridge, Mass.: Harvard University Press, Twelfth Printing, 1972), p. 984, col. 1, #6707, item 9; Joseph Edkins, *The Evolution of the Chinese Language* (London: Trubner and Co., 1888), p. v; Hsin Cheng Yu, *Ancient Chinese History* (Taiwan Commercial Press, 1963), p. 6.

4. W. A. P. Martin, *The Lore of Cathay* (London: Oliphant, Anderson and Ferrier, 1901), pp. 165 - 198.

5. James Legge, *The Notions of the Chinese Concerning God and Spirits* (Hong Kong: Hong Kong Register Office, 1852), p. 50.

6. Legge, p. 28.

7. Legge, p. 28.

8. Legge, p. 29.

9. W. J. Clennell, *The Historical Development of Religion in China* (London: The Theosophical Publishing House, Ltd., 1917), pp. 19 - 32.

10. Audrey Topping, "China's Incredible Find," *National Geographic Magazine*, 153 (April 1978), pp. 440-459.

11. Ibid., pp. 440 - 459.

12. Regis, *Yih-king*, Vol. II, p. 411.

13. Legge, pp. 46, 47.

14. Legge, p. 44.

15. Legge, p. 7.

16. Legge, p. 32.

17. Note the interesting phonetic similarities in *Shen* 神 ; *ShangTi* 上帝 (also pronounced *"Shangdai"*); *Sheng* 聖 and the Hebrew term for *the Almighty*, "Shaddai" (as used in Genesis 17:1, Psalm 91:1, for example). It is possible these words *Shang*, *Sheng*, and *Shen* may have originally been identical in pronunciation.

Chapter 3: Easy Lessons in "Character Building"

1. R. H. Mathews, *Chinese-English Dictionary* (Cambridge, Mass.: Harvard University Press, Twelfth Printing, 1972). All radical number references throughout the book.

2. *Korea--Its Land, People and Culture of All Ages* (Seoul: HakwonSa Ltd., 1960), pp. 114-118. See also *Worldmark Encyclopedia of Nations* (New York: Harper & Row, Fourth Edition, Vol. 4, 1971), pp. 176, 184; G. Bourgois, *Dictionary and Glossary for the Practical Study of the Japanese Ideographs* (Yokohama: Tokyo-Kyo Bun Kwan), p. xviii.

3. James H. Shultz, "The Christian Church in T'ang China" (Los Angeles: A thesis presented to the Faculty of the Graduate School, University of Southern California, 1970), pp. 17, 25, 35.

4. Robert K. Douglas, *The Language and Literature of China* (London: Trubner and Co., 1875), pp. 18-27.

5. Since this is such a debatable point and the whole logic of the hypothesis for the book revolves about the classification of many characters as ideographic instead of phonetic, additional arguments will be here offered.

There are many radical combinations that have become phonetic. However, it is only logical to assume that the *first* use of a radical combination must have been ideographic, or the radicals would never have been combined in the first place. Once the radicals had been brought together and had a certain phonetic sound attached (taken from the original ideograph), they then became a phonetic set, and could be used to form other characters by phonetic sense only. If one examines all the characters listed phonetically carrying the same radical combination, *the original must be the ideogram.*

For example, let us examine the characters listed in Mathew's *Chinese-English Dictionary* under "fu," *to fill, a roll of cloth* 畐 . This radical combination by itself does not appear to be ideographic. One would deduce that originally it must have been part of a larger ideographic character. Then there is *to fall prostrate, to crawl on hands and knees* 匐 (not ideographic); *a strip of cloth, a hem or border* 幅 (also not ideographic). *Happiness, prosperity, good fortune* 福 is a character which can be analyzed ideographically, if one were familiar with primeval history as revealed in sacred Scriptures. The first *happiness* known to man was *God's* 礻 gift to the *first* 一 *person* 口 (Adam) *of landed property, the Garden* 田 of Eden. It is logical to deduce, therefore, that the radical combination "fu" 畐 originated in this ideographic character for *happiness* (which incidentally is a very ancient and simple character).

happiness

Furthermore, *a bat* 蝠 (also used as an emblem of *happiness*, from the sound), is obviously a phonetic character formed on the basis of 福 and would also contribute to the theory that 福 was the original combination.

Many characters may appear to be phonetic if one is not acquainted with the historical basis of the formation of the ideograph. Hence, if in truth, many characters are based on a common knowledge of historical fact, one not acquainted with the Biblical Genesis would not be in a position to interpret them.

Looking at the language purely from a phonetic viewpoint it would appear that some words were either given the same "sound" as intentional inventions, or naturally evolved in the course of developing spoken language, since they concern closely related subjects. Many words doubtless began as "slang" or colloquial expressions. Let us examine an English illustration first, the word, AIR. Originally this word must have indicated the atmospheric gas which one breathes. To *air* something out, means to freshen it in the *air*, or dry it out; an *air* can be melody or tune (possibly originally whistled into the *air*); one can *air* or publicize an opinion (in the open); one can go on the *air* (broadcast by radio waves); something in the *air* is about to happen, but is not yet apparent; one can be up in the *air* and be unsettled or angry; or one can walk on *air* and be happy and exuberant. Thus the phonetic sound, AIR, can take on a multitude of meanings, but all can be obviously and meaning fully derived from an original simple word association.

In like manner, is it not conceivable that the same phonetic sound in Chinese can be equated with related subjects? For example the word "T'IEN": perhaps originally "t'ien" indicated *heaven* 天 and was therefore also equated with *God*, the *Heavenly Ruler* or *Shang-Ti*. The first meeting place of God with man was the *Garden* (t'ien) 田 of Eden, the home of the first lords of the earth, Adam and Eve. Thus, it is plausible that the home of the earthly ruler, or the *imperial domain* (tien) 甸 came to be called the same. It was in the *Garden* 田 where man met face to face with God and was also *ashamed* (t'ien) 靦 because of the *law and statute* (tien) 典 that Adam and Eve first broke. They doubtless built an altar at the gate of the Garden after they were expelled so that the *Garden* (t'ien) 田 became associated with worship. Later when a *temple* 殿 was erected, it too became a "tien". "Tien" also came to mean an *offering of libation* 奠. Finally, "tien" 點 is a *dot* or a *point* which consecrates or anoints. For example the character *king* 王 is "dotted" 主 and becomes *lord*. The addition of this *dot* on an ancestral tablet in the temple was a service of consecration.

Thus it can be seen that both ideographic and phonetic relationships may naturally develop without any stretch of the imagination, but again, a knowledge of Genesis history is necessary to understand the interrelationship of words.

6. Bradley Smith and Wan-go Weng, *China, A History in Art* (New York: Doubleday, 1972), pp. 26, 27.

7. Smith and Weng, p. 10.

8. Smith and Weng, p. 33.

9. H. T. Morgan, *Chinese Symbols and Superstitions* (Los Angeles: Times - Mirror Printing and Binding House, 1942), pp. 27, 28.

10. G. D. Wilder and J. H. Ingram, *Analysis of Chinese Characters* (Taipei: Chin Wen Publ. Co., 1964), pp. iv-vi.

Chapter 4: Creation — Chinese Style

1. In the Old Testament the "former and latter rains," necessary for bringing the crops to fruition, are com-

pared with the pouring out of God's Spirit upon the earth, which in turn promotes spiritual growth: "For he has given the early rain for your vindication. ... The early and the latter rain, as before ... And it shall come to pass afterward, that I will pour out my Spirit on all flesh" (Joel 2 : 23, 28).

2. 工 in more ancient forms is written 𝕀 , 𝕀 , 𝕫 , so that there is no question that the vertical stroke represents a *man* | with *hair* 彡 in the first figure, an *arm* ト in the second, and *bending* 𝉔 in the third.

3. 靈 anciently was written as 霝 , an exact duplication. Also note this significant form: 㸑 , which will become more significant if reviewed after the entire book is read.

Spirit (ancient form)

4. The "p'ieh" ノ appears to be written as ∪ in many earlier figures. Note 告 becomes 𝉔 .

5. 造 = 𝉔 , 𝉔 , 𝉔 .

6. 先 = 𝉔

7. When Moses met with God on Mount Sinai, he become "a mirror of His glory," for upon returning to speak to the Israelites, they could not bear to look upon the glory of his face. "And when he descended he did not know that *the skin of his face shone* because he had been speaking with the Lord. ... Whenever the skin of Moses' face shone in the sight of the Israelites, he would put the veil back over his face until he went in again to speak with the Lord"(Exodus 34 : 29, 35, NEB).

8. 西 = ⊗ , where ト is a *man* and ⊗ is a *garden* 田 . A second figure, 𝉔 , represents a *person, alone* 厶 , by 𝉔 (right half of 𝉔). Often figures are elongated to enclose the lower radical in the ancient forms.

*happiness
(ancient
form)*

9. 福 = 福 . In some ancient forms ⌐ is clearly a *house or roof* ∩ or ∧ . Also the one ⊡ becomes *two persons* 自 , 自 in 𓉞 and 𓊝 (see p. 52).

Chapter 5: They Shall Be One Flesh

1. 要 = 𓏲 . In this primitive character, an even clearer picture is seen with (God's) *hands* ╞╡ placing a *man* | in the *garden* ⊗ . Below is the *woman* 㕚 . Other ancient forms have omitted the garden enclosure but emphasized the *two people* 㑊 , 㑊 (see 呂 p. 48 and 且 p. 52).

2. *To enter* 入 and *flesh* 肉 both carry the sound "ju," and are equally primitive radicals (11 and 130, respectively). Their phonetic similarity (remembering that the spoken language preceded the written) strongly suggests that *to enter* was closely associated in the ancient Chinese mind with the creation of Eve ("flesh of my flesh") from the "entering" of Adam's chest.

*gold
(ancient
form)*

3. The ⌄ in 金 becomes clear in the more primitive forms: 㝵 , 㝵 , which depict two *fiery persons* 炎 . That these *fires* truly represent two persons is verified by 㝵 where ∘∘ indicate two *mouths* (persons). Bdellium is defined as any deep red gem, especially a garnet, while onyx is a variety of agate with alternate layers of color.

4. The ancient form 朿 for 來 leaves no doubt that 人人 represents *two persons.*

5. This is more clearly depicted in the earlier calligraphy, 㑊 , where 𠂉 is 彳 ; 朿 shows a *man* ⃒ superimposed on *heaven, sea and land* 𡈼 *(a lord)* in three horizontal positions; and ㇒ represents the action of *walking.*

*to go
(ancient
form)*

6. 從 = 𨑔

7. 僉 = 僉 . The two *mouths* ㅂㅂ are obviously a part of the two *persons* 🅈🅈 (and not four persons).

8. 仁 = 仆 , 弖 , 仨 .

9. 圍 = 圉 , 圉 . The bottom figure 夊 , 〜 , 〜 will become even more apparent as *two persons* in Chapter 7.

Chapter 6: The Fruit Tragedy

1. 鬼 = 鬼 , 鬼

2. 魂 = 魂 . Note that 厶 *(secretly, privately, alone)* is used in reference to the *speaking* 云 as well as descriptive of the *devil's* 鬼 activity.

soul
(ancient form)

Chapter 7: Dust to Dust

1. 裸 is portrayed clearly in 裸 as a *covering* 〜 of fruit 果 on *two persons* 〜 .

2. 苦 = 苦 .

naked
(ancient form)

3. 罰 = 罰 , 罰 , 罰 .

4. 衰 = 衰 , 衰 , 衰 .

to fine
(ancient form)

Chapter 8: The Seed of Rebellion

1. William F. Beck, *The Holy Bible*, An American Translation. See also Martin Luther's German translation of the Bible, "Ich habe den Mann, den Herrn." (I have the Man [or that Man], the Lord.)

2. Compare the experiences of Gideon (Judges 6:2), Elijah on Mount Carmel (1 Kings 18:36-38), or Solomon at the dedication of the temple (2 Chronicles 7:1), when their offerings were consumed by fire from heaven.

3. 後 = 㣟 . In this earlier figure, Adam and Eve are depicted by 丿 (彳). The rest of the character, 㐆 , depicts a series of *persons* 口 . 夂 is a *person* 𠆢 on the side. The vertical line through it could indicate the continuation of begetting . . . etc.

4. John Ross, *The Original Religion of China* (London: Oliphant, Anderson and Ferrier, 1909), p. 212.

5. Ross, p. 212.

6. Other forms of 祀, such as 祘 , might account for the lesser seal writing, 祀 , and the current symbol 祀. But what does 㠯 represent? Could it be the smoke curling up from the offering, with *two persons* 从 standing on either side 祘 ?

7. Amenhotep IV (Akhenaton) was a single exception. He attempted to overthrow Egypt's polytheistic religion by substituting the worship of only Aton, the sun god (who was still a false god). He founded a new capital near Tell el Amarna, but his rule lasted only 10 years, following which the government of Egypt returned to Thebes and their old gods. [Lionel Casson, *Ancient Egypt* (New York: Time Incorporated, 1965), p. 59.]

8. W. A. P. Martin, *The Lore of Cathay or the Intellect of China* (London: Oliphant, Anderson and Ferrier, 1901), p. 167.

9. Ross, p. 296.

Chapter 9: A Bleak World

1. Immanuel Velikovsky, *Worlds in Collision* (Garden City, N. Y.: Doubleday & Co., 1950), p. 380. See also Donald W. Patten, *The Biblical Flood and the Ice Epoch* (Seattle: Pacific Meridian Publ. Co., 1966), p. 64

2. It is claimed by some that 船 is a "modern" character, not more than 2,000 years old, since it was not found in the *Shuo Wen*. For examples see: G. D. Wilder, and J. H. Ingram, *Analysis of Chinese Characters* (Taipei: Chin Wen Publ. Co., 1964), pp. 118, 119. However, because 船 fails to appear in this ancient etymological study cannot be used as final evidence. In the light of of Genesis, the character is ideographic -- why should its originator use *eight* 八 *persons* 口 ? The phonetic set, 㕣 , *a marsh at the foot of the hills*, is not by itself ideographic, and therefore must be a part of a larger original ideogram. 沿 meaning *to follow a course, to coast, to hand down, to continue*, also contains this radical set, but is not in itself ideographic. 㕣 and 沿 are both phonetically "yen," while 船 is "chuan." Therefore 㕣 is not a phonetic in 船. Ancient forms of 船 are 𦩍 or 𦩍 , having very clearly "eight persons." It would seem that logically 船 is the true and, very possibly, the original ideogram.

3. 濬 = 濬 .

4. 共 = 𦥑 , 廾 , 鬩 . In this last figure eight helping hands are seen contained within a larger mirror-image figure *eight* ﹛﹜.

5. 祭. The Korean character for this word is clearly 祭 (with 又 instead of ㇇). Earlier forms show a *hand* 𠂇 instead of *again* 又 . Some interesting phonetic

*total
(ancient
form)*

similarities are observed: to *sacrifice* 祭; *a border, boundary* 際 (阝 meaning *a mound*), are "chi"; and *to pray, beseech* 祈 and *boundary, border* 圻 are "ch'i." Doubtless the words all arose phonetically from the services of *praying* at the *border sacrifices*. It is interesting that 阝 is *mound*, and the shape of 圡 also suggests a brick *(earth)* elevation. See description of the T'ien Tan (p. 91).

Chapter 10: Tower of United Defiance

1. Will Durant, *The Story of Civilization: Our Oriental Heritage* (New York: Simon and Schuster, 1942), pp. 224, 225.

2. Durant, p. 741.

3. L in the earlier calligraphy is seen as 乚 (right half of 儿), a form of 儿.

4. 舌 = 舌 , 舌 .

to scatter (ancient form)

5. 散 = 𢿭 . In this ancient writing. 𠕋 is clearly *flesh* 月; the 𣫭 may represent *four* ⅠⅠⅠⅠ persons holding up *hands* (the males?) and may be comparable with an ancient figure for *all* 共, written as 𠔽 , which shows four intertwining, united hands.

6. Note how this radical for *west* 西 is greatly compacted in this character taken from p. 109 遷. Compare this with the character *desire, necessary* 要. The radical *four* 四 receives similar treatment, in *to punish* 罰.

Epilog . . . Revelation

1. ⊞ is square in the present calligraphy, and in the majority of earlier forms usually maintains this configuration ⊕ , ⊕ . However, occasionally it may be stylized as round or oval, ⊕ , ⊗ . The "rivers" may be horizontal and vertical as depicted above, diagonal ⊗ , "meandering" ⊕ , or even more stylized as ⊗ or ⊗ .

BIBLIOGRAPHY

Alexander, George and Dart, John. "Tablets Shed New Light on the Bible." *Los Angeles Times*, June, 7, 1976.

Blakney, Raymond B. *A Course in the Analysis of Chinese Characters*. Shanghai: The Commercial Press, Ltd., 1926.

Bourgois, G. *Dictionary and Glossary for the Practical Study of the Japanese Ideographs*. Yokohama: Tokyo-Kyo Bun Kwan., n.d.

Broomhall, Marshall. *The Bible in China*. London: British & Foreign Bible Society, 1934.

Casson, Lionel. *Ancient Egypt*. New York: Time Incorp., 1965.

Clennell, W. J. *The Historical Development of Religion in China*. London: The Theosophical Publishing House, Ltd., 1917.

Coffin, Harold G. *Creation — Accident or Design?* Washington, D. C.: Review and Herald Publ. Assoc., 1969.

Darwin, Charles. *The Origin of Species by Natural Selection*. New York: D. Appleton & Co., 1860.

de Camp, L. Sprague. *The Great Monkey Trial*. Garden City, N. Y. : Doubleday & Co., 1968.

de Groot, J. J. M. *Religion in China*. New York: Knickerbocker Press, 1912.

de Groot, J. J. M. *The Religion of the Chinese*. New York: MacMillan, 1910.

De La Couperie, Terrien. *The Language of China Before the Chinese*. Taipei: Ch'eng-wen Publishing Co., 1966.

Douglas, Robert K. *The Language and Literature of China.* London: Trubner and Co., 1875.

Du Ponceau, Peter S. *A Dissertation on the Nature and Character of the Chinese System of Writing.* Philadelphia: Published for the American Philosophical Society by McCarty and Davis, 1838.

Durant, Will. *The Story of Civilization: Our Oriental Heritage.* New York: Simon and Schuster, 1942.

Edkins, Joseph. *The Evolution of the Chinese Language.* London: Trubner and Co., 1888.

Hsin Cheng Yu. *Ancient Chinese History.* Taiwan Commercial Press., 1964.

Hughes, E. R. *Religion in China.* London: William Brendon & Son, Ltd., 1950.

Korea-It's Land, People and Culture of All Ages. Seoul: Hakwon-Sa Ltd., 1960.

Legge, James. *The Notions of the Chinese Concerning God and Spirits.* Hong Kong: Hong Kong Register Office, 1852.

Lin Tze Ching, *Ting Jung Liu Shui Tong.* Nanking: Quang Ee, China, 1973.

Lo Hsiang Lin. *Authorized High Middle School History of China.* Peking: Republic of China Education Department, 1936.

Martin, W.A.P. *The Lore of Cathay or The Intellect of China.* London: Oliphant, Anderson & Ferrier, 1901.

Mathews, R.H. *Chinese-English Dictionary.* Cambridge, Mass: Harvard University Press, Twelfth Printing, 1972.

Morgan, H. T. *Chinese Symbols and Superstitions.* Los Angeles: Times-Mirror Printing and Binding House, 1942.

Noorbergen, Rene. *The Ark File.* Mountain View: Pacific Press Publishing Assoc., 1974.

Parker, E. H. *Studies in Chinese Religion.* London: Chapman & Hall, Ltd., 1910.

Patten, Donald W. *The Biblical Flood and the Ice Epoch.* Seattle: Pacific Meridian Publishing Co., 1966.

Pettinato, Giovanni. "The Royal Archives of Tell Mardikh-Ebla," *Biblical Archaeologist* 39 (1976).

Plopper, Clifford H. *Chinese Religion Seen Through the Proverb.* Shanghai: The China Press, 1926.

Rawley, H. H. *Prophecy and Religion in Ancient China and Israel.* New York: Harper & Row, 1952.

Reese, Edward and Klassen, Frank R. *The Chronological Bible.* Nashville; Regal Publishers, Inc., 1977.

Regis. *Yih-king.* Vol. II. n.d.

Ritland, Richard M. *A Search for Meaning in Nature.* Mountain View: Pacific Press Publishing Assoc., 1970.

Ross, John. *The Original Religion of China.* London: Oliphant Anderson & Ferrier, 1909.

Sanderson, Ivan T. "Riddle of the Quick-Frozen Giants," *Saturday Evening Post*, Jan. 16, 1960.

Schultz, James H. "The Christian Church in T'ang China," Los Angeles: A Thesis presented to the Faculty of the Graduate School, University of Southern California, 1970.

Smith, Bradley and Weng, Wan-go. *China, A History in Art.* New York: Doubleday, 1972.

Susuma, Ohno. *The Origin of the Japanese Language*. Tokyo : Kokusai Bunka Shinkokai (Japan Cultural Society), 1970.

Topping, Audrey. "China's Incredible Find." *National Geographic Magazine*, 153 (April 1978).

Velikovsky, Immanuel, *Worlds in Collision*. Garden City, N. Y.: Doubleday & Co., 1950.

Werner, E. T. C. *Myths and Legends of China*. London: George G. Harrop & Co., 1922.

Wieger, Leo. *A History of the Religious Beliefs and Philosophical Opinions of China*. Hsien : Hsien Press, China, 1927.

Wilder, G. D., and Ingram, J. H. *Analysis of Chinese Characters*. Taipei: Chin Wen Publishing Co., 1964.

Worldmark Encyclopedia of Nations. Vol. 4. New York: Harper & Row, 1971.

Yamauchi Edwin. *The Stones and the Scriptures*. Philadelphia: J. B. Lippincott Co., 1972.

Yuen Ren Chao. *Language and Symbolic Systems*. Cambridge: Cambridge University Press., 1960.